# PRAISE FO

# disentangle

"*Disentangle* is an extremely valuable guidebook for people in difficult family/divorce/matrimonial law disputes. I encourage couples to use this guide not to win their case, but to learn how to win their lives back in a positive, non-adversarial way. Long after the court case is over, the parties have to find ways to co-parent, coexist, and move on to the next best possibility. Until they disentangle, it is all but impossible.

"*Disentangle* is also a valuable guide for matrimonial attorneys to read in order to give the best counsel to their clients involved in personal misery cases. Many of my family law attorneys have reported that it has helped them get their clients focused on their lives in a healthier way and move away from the personal pain matters for which the courts are unlikely and unable to provide relief to the parties."

**Hon. Joseph Moody Buckner**
Chief District Judge
Hillsborough, North Carolina

"Nancy Johnston's *Disentangle* is an exceptionally clear and accessible handbook for doing just that: disentangling from the life patterns that hold us hostage. It's also a guide for moving on, with a wealth of good counsel on setting healthy boundaries. Favorite chapter: 'Developing Spirituality,' which is both inspiring and utterly practical. Bravo!"

**Lisa Tracy**
Journalist and Author of *Objects of Our
Affection: Uncovering My Family's Past,
One Chair, Pistol, and Pickle Fork at a Time*

"By offering her own experience, strength, and hope, Nancy Johnston provides practical solutions to all of us who struggle with separating ourselves from others in a loving way. In her book, *Disentangle: When You've Lost Your Self in Someone Else,* I find methods and tools for setting healthy boundaries, recognizing when those boundaries have been crossed, and living peacefully with people and circumstances over which I have no control. At the same time, the book provides guidance on developing and strengthening the person I am and the person I want to become. When I'm out of balance and recognize that I'm tumbling into an entanglement, I can turn to this book for help. I am grateful for Nancy's wisdom, honesty, and generosity; her words speak to my heart and guide my spirit."

**Hope L. Hennessey**
Editor and Life Coach

"The moment I laid eyes on Nancy Johnston's subtitle, *When You've Lost Your Self in Someone Else,* I knew that this author understood the process of loss, and I also knew from the title, *Disentangle,* that she had identified a path out. Immediately I began putting her four-pronged approach (Facing Illusions, Detaching, Setting Healthy Boundaries, and Developing Spirituality) to work in my own life. Next I introduced these concepts to my clients, especially my weekly Boundaries Group. What a wonderful guidebook!

"I love the way the book is formatted, with a near perfect balance of vulnerability and self-disclosure, client stories, and practical skills. I strongly recommend *Disentangle* to anyone in recovery, those professionals working with others in recovery, and anyone whose relationships are entangled."

**Margaret L. Cress, LMFT**

"As an experiential educator who works closely with individuals to help them deal with life's struggles, fears, and changes, this book's amazing value has been realized by me many times. In the last several years, I have purchased and given this book to close relatives, colleagues, and my ex-wife.

"A colleague of mine struggled for years with her son's drug addiction. Before receiving *Disentangle* she always gave in to the charms of her son and his promises to stop drugs, do better, and get his life together. She gave him money and unconditional love only to have her hopes dashed each time. Now, based in part on Nancy's book, she has been able to step back and set boundaries that protect her from the awful hurt she has endured for years."

**Russ Watkins**
Owner/Director
ASCEND

"Nancy has created a combination resource/workbook for all of those who have struggled with 'losing themselves' when in a relationship with a partner, parent, child, friend, or coworker. Any who have benefited from classic codependency books such as *Codependent No More* by Melody Beattie, *Women Who Love Too Much* by Robin Norwood, *Getting Them Sober* by Toby Rice Drews, or *Facing Codependency* by Pia Mellody, will find Nancy's book a step-by-step method to put what they have learned to work and apply it specifically to their situations. *Disentangle* is written from Nancy's wisdom gleaned from years as a therapist, as well as personal experience in her own relationships. I have found it more user-friendly than most self-help books, and I recommend it to other therapists as a resource for clients. It's also a great supplement to any twelve-step program. Thanks for this great addition to relationship resources, Nancy!"

**Lois Horne, Ed.S., LPC, LSATP**

"This very useful book helped me to disentangle from an alcoholic and verbally abusive husband. I have written nineteen books, and I heartily endorse Johnston's book and her methods, which have helped me to move on into a wholesome and very happy new relationship."

**Katie Letcher Lyle**
Author

"A practical, easy-reading guide to codependency, the behavior set first recognized in those living with and around alcoholics and addicts. Using stories from her experiences, Johnston accurately outlines not only the issues of codependency, but also the spiritual tools necessary to unravel the mess created by these behaviors in life's relationships. The book is a highly valuable read for anyone with a personal or clinical interest in the problems of codependency."

**David L. Nelson, MD**

"*Disentangle* is a reader-friendly self-help manual filled with ideas about how to build a more self-directed, peaceful life. It is a 'must have' for anyone entering recovery with codependency issues. Setting healthy boundaries is a learned behavior that demands practice, and Ms. Johnston discusses in detail how to begin this process in a thoughtful manner. Johnston's ability to empower readers to apply these concepts to themselves makes this book an essential part of any bibliotherapy. Practitioners or graduate students who are motivated to deepen self-awareness will also find this book a good companion on that journey."

**Rana Duncan-Daston, LCSW, Ed.D.**
Radford University School of Social Work

disentangle

Nancy L. Johnston, MS, LPC, LSATP

# disentangle

## When You've Lost Your Self
## in Someone Else

**Central Recovery Press**

Las Vegas, Nevada

CENTRAL RECOVERY PRESS

## CENTRAL RECOVERY PRESS

Central Recovery Press (CRP) is committed to publishing exceptional materials addressing addiction treatment, recovery, and behavioral health care, including original and quality books, audio/visual communications, and Web-based new media. Through a diverse selection of titles, it seeks to impact the behavioral health care field with a broad range of unique resources for professionals, recovering individuals, and their families.

For more information, visit www.centralrecoverypress.com.

Central Recovery Press, Las Vegas, NV 89129
© 2003, 2011 by Nancy L. Johnston

ISBN-13: 978-1-936290-03-1
ISBN-10: 1-936290-03-0

Publisher:   Central Recovery Press
             3371 N. Buffalo Drive
             Las Vegas, NV 89129

**Editor's Note:** *Disentangle* is designed to provide accurate and valuable information about the subject matter presented. The material and approach come from the author's personal history, as well as her work as a psychotherapist over more than three decades. However, it is in no way intended to serve as a substitute for professional behavioral health care services. In the event that such services are needed, a licensed professional should be consulted.

*Cover design and interior by Sara Streifel, Think Creative Design*
*Photo of Nancy Johnston by Grace DuVal Johnston*

# Table of Contents

# living

disentangle

"I am well and strong. And so is *Disentangle*."

# Preface to the Revised Edition

Many seasons have passed since I wrote the first Preface. Much water has flowed down our river. Many walks along it have occurred. Many trips down the river on tubes and in canoes have been enjoyed. Our children have been raised and are now out in the much bigger world. We have aged and wear glasses and get discounts for being senior citizens. We are well and strong.

I am well and strong. And so is *Disentangle*.

In fact, *Disentangle* has reached such a level of good health that a dream of mine has come true: *Disentangle* has been picked up by a traditional, a.k.a. "real," publisher, and I am very pleased to say that it is Central Recovery Press (CRP). You know that already, because if you now have the book in your hands and are reading this, it has been released by CRP. This is a major success for me and my book.

It has been seven years since I wrote the first Preface after walking with my friend, Sally, along the river. That day we were speaking about my releasing the book through various forms of self-publishing. Much has happened with *Disentangle* since that day to develop and support the book's success and bring it into this broader, professional market. There are many stories and people along the way who have supported and fostered the growth of this project, and to each of them I am extremely grateful. And I am amazed at how this book and its contents have blossomed into more ideas, tools, and opportunities. Here is some of this story over these years.

When I finished writing *Disentangle,* I sent it to several traditional publishers for consideration for publication. One publisher expressed strong interest in it twice but never chose to accept it. I found their near-acceptance encouraging, and, of course, I believed strongly in the value of this material, so I pursued self-publication. I let go of the desire and need to have someone else publish the book and went about my business of helping to relay and teach this information to interested others.

Initially the book was printed by an office supply store and had a plastic spiral binding. A local bookstore owner was more than willing to put it on her shelves, and we had a successful book signing for the public. People bought it in her store and in my office. I realized that the form of the book easily lent itself to conducting workshops on it, and I began to do just that in my office as an additional aspect of my clinical practice. All sorts of individuals found the book and came to these workshops. I started to see that what I anticipated was true—the book has broad appeal and application. The list of people I write about on the second page of the book are the people who were drawn in by its title and who became excited about the way the *Disentangle* approach is constructed.

By March 2004 I had upgraded the form of the book by working with a professional self-publishing company that helped me to design and construct a bound copy of the book that could be ordered on demand. That worked very well, and over these years around 1,200 copies of *Disentangle* have been sold in that self-published version. The local bookstore owner again sponsored a book signing for this new release, and interest from readers continued to show up, individual by individual.

With a professionally bound book in my hands and a history of conducting workshops based on its concepts, tools, and techniques, I decided to branch out beyond my wonderful and receptive community to the broader world. I was accepted to present some of the book's material at a statewide conference. The response by attendees was very strong—so strong that I was surprised. I had standing room only in the session, sold all of the books I had brought, and had a number of people speaking with me after the session. One person in particular, who worked in an employee assistance program (EAP) setting, was so positive and eager for the material in *Disentangle* that she connected me with a regional EAP conference at which I presented shortly thereafter.

I presented the *Disentangle* approach at numerous other conferences over the next three to four years. I learned that one successful presentation builds on another, that I would meet people at one conference who would connect me with another opportunity to present. I presented to mental health counselors, addiction counselors, guidance counselors, EAP counselors, doctors, nurses, and unit staff for hospitals, treatment centers, and prisons.

Now I don't want to sound like I was out on a full-time lecture or presentation circuit by any means. At the most, I would present five to six times per year at various and wonderful places on the East Coast. I continued to be a full-time counselor in my private practice, a mother, and a wife. I had no agent or staff, and so I did what I could produce by my self. And it was plenty.

As I said above, I was surprised by the strong and positive interest in *Disentangle* at these presentations. I know the importance of its material both personally and professionally. Importance is actually an understatement. Imperative is more the word for me; to be able to disentangle is imperative for my serenity and growth. It was true then when I wrote the book; it is still true now. But what I have been writing about and presenting on is known generally as "codependence," and that word and its meaning can be controversial and often misunderstood. Thus, when I find out that my workshops and presentations are full even though I am not a "known" presenter, I realize that the topics of codependence and tangled relationships have brought people into the room. I am very glad about that. We may not want to look at our relationship tangles, our codependence, but not doing so leaves us vulnerable to others and to our self in a chronically unhealthy way.

In doing these workshops and presentations, I found another way to apply the material in *Disentangle*—I have used it to help my self as a presenter and teacher. I have had to see the reality of how much I can and cannot present in a workshop or conference session, the reality of how people may or may not respond to the material, and the reality of how the session may or may not go as planned. I have used detachment to listen and observe when people are expressing a view or idea different from mine. I constantly have to employ boundaries as I consider the time allotted for the session and the material I have to present. And spirituality is there with me as I deal with my anxiety about being up in front of people, as I let go of my attachment to wanting to make something happen for each person there, and as I settle into the flow of when and where I will be asked to present again, not forcing solutions but doing my part and letting go.

Now Central Recovery Press has made it possible for *you* to have this book, for it to be available to a much broader world. How did this happen? Through the flow of life, of course. I was simply minding my business in the fall of 2009, seeing clients and returning phone calls. One of those calls was a client wanting some information about the use of medications to treat addictions. I said I had just seen an article in a professional magazine on this topic. I said I would look it up and get back with the client about that information. I immediately did so. In the process of looking through the magazine, I found an announcement about Central Recovery Treatment and specifically about Central Recovery Press. I thought, "I don't know this press. What is this press about?" I made a note to look it up on the Internet that night. And I did.

I was immediately excited about the possibility of submitting *Disentangle* to them for consideration for publication. I had not done such a submission since the early years of the book. I was not looking for a publisher. I had just gone ahead with my work and with my work with the book over those years. And then, when the time was right and when I was ready, the publisher appeared and accepted.

Thanks to Central Recovery Press's willingness to publish *Disentangle* and the excellent support and guidance of my editors there, Nancy Schenck and Dan Mager, you too are now in the flow of this project, a project that offers each of us the opportunity to not lose our self in someone else but rather to connect with our self, strengthen our self, interact with others in ways healthier for our self, and gain greater serenity for our self.

Yesterday I was again tubing on the river with my husband and some of our close friends, among them Sally. And once again, at the end of our ride down the river, we were walking back on the river path carrying our tubes and talking about the soon-to-be release of *Disentangle* by Central Recovery Press. As my husband and friends spoke with me about this wonderful evolution of the book, I felt their love and support. And I felt my own love and support, grateful for all that I am learning, and loving the flow of the river and of my life.

*Nancy L. Johnston*
*July, 2010*

"I was glad to be where I was, knew where I was going, and felt very content."

# Preface to the First Edition

Recently I took a walk with a good friend of mine along the river that runs by our homes. We were walking our dogs and talking about the final stages of this book. She has been very interested in and supportive of this project. Over its development we have talked about its contents and their applicability to our lives. We continue to do so. We are also now talking about the details of putting it into print and distributing it beyond our community.

As we sat on a fallen tree and watched the river flow by, I reflected on what a life project this has been for me. As you will find in reading *Disentangle*, it has evolved as I have evolved. There were times when I truly felt lost in someone else, as though I was lost in the woods. I would feel terribly overwhelmed by the situation with this other person and have no idea what to do about it or how to help my self find my way back to my own security and peace of mind.

I have chosen to use the picture of the tree on the front of this book for at least a couple of reasons known to me. The tree is in my front yard and is positioned outside the window out of which I look as I have written this book. It has been my constant companion and has endured many seasons, as has the writing of this book that now totals eight years in the making. I have also chosen to use the picture of the tree because it represents both lostness in the woods and the finding of our way out of the woods, as suggested by the light shining through the expanding branches. I have learned that by applying the ideas of disentangling to my life, I experience the same type of openings, expansions, and light, and in so doing, I find my self and am no longer lost.

As you may have already noticed in my writing here, I am separating the word "self" from possessives such as "my" and "your." This is intentional on my part. I want to emphasize the word "self." It is, in fact, what this book is largely about, and I am interested in helping the reader to keep that word, that concept, that important reality in mind. *Disentangle* is about finding our self when we have lost it in someone else. It is about learning how to connect with our self and then knowing how to respond to it in ways that make us stronger, clearer, and more serene.

I find my self unable or unwilling to try to express specific acknowledgments for help with this book, and I choose not to dedicate it to any one person. So many people have been involved in my life and in the writing of this book, both directly and indirectly, that I could not adequately list them, thank them, or offer a narrowed dedication.

With this in mind, I will say that this book is gratefully offered by me to each of you who have an interest in making your life better by taking the time and energy to look at your self and make the changes that will help you to be centered and happier as you interact with people in your life. This book is not about changing them. It's about changing you so that you can enjoy life, others, and especially your self.

And so, my friend and I continued on our walk by the river, leaving the fallen tree and making our way back to the path through the woods. The dogs knew the way home, and so did we. The path was fresh and clear. Our spirits were bright and energized. I was glad to be where I was, knew where I was going, and felt very content.

I trust that the ideas in this book can similarly offer each of us a path to a peaceful and centered self.

*Nancy L. Johnston*
*January, 2003*

**Please note:** *Interspersed throughout* Disentangle *you will find experiential exercises that provide valuable opportunities to practice applying the material to your life. I encourage you to complete these exercises in a separate journal. They will help you expand your awareness and build skills toward healthier relationships with others, and with your self.*

Every damn time I get in a relationship, I am no longer me.

He melts me. He has this sick hold on me.

The last eight years are

a haze—like I didn't

exist in my own right.

I do not like who I am with him.

As years went on,

I slowly lost my

identity. I gave up

things I loved to do.

I felt like I gave my self away.

I attach my self to the person . . . .
that relationship is first and foremost.

I would give anything to be the person he wants to be with.

It just wore me down.

# tangles

(as described by various people along the way)

I don't understand why I so readily gave up my self for her.

I can't seem to get back to me.

When he left me, I was distraught in a major way and was helpless to know what to do.

I don't know who the hell I am anymore.

I'm not me when I'm around him.

I'm losing who I was before I met her.

"I can't seem to get back to me."

# 1 By Definition

*Disentangle: To find your self when you are lost in someone else. To create enough emotional space between your self and another person so you are better able to see the realities of your situation and make healthier decisions about it. To not necessarily leave/divorce/end a relationship but rather create enough space and establish a stronger self so you can then decide what to do about the relationship in which you are entangled.*

When we are emotionally overinvolved with another person, we lose our self and our way. Our thoughts become focused on that other person whether we want them to be or not. Sometimes we may justify those thoughts, believing that if we don't worry about the other person, fix things for him or her, plan his or her life, or do what he or she asks of us, then things will just be terrible. Sometimes those thoughts become paralyzing. We feel that we can think of nothing else, that we must immediately do something to be in contact with that other person to impact his or her life (and our life, of course, though we do not necessarily see that at first). We feel awful. We are nervous, anxious, agitated. We set aside important work. We set aside important people. We set aside our self.

As the entanglements progress, we lose our way out. Our interactions with the other person become more complicated, more confusing, more frustrating, more angry. We believe that more of this same behavior on our part of trying to explain and resolve a given problem will produce the results we desire. So we continue on and on. And things get worse for all. Everyone is upset and no one is getting what they think they want. We are entangled.

Entanglements can happen in various relationships. We may be entangled with our spouse, our parents, our children, our bosses. We can become entangled with clerks in stores and telephone operators for insurance companies and other businesses. An entanglement occurs with anyone with whom we lose our centeredness in our interactions with him or her. We don't have to be related to the person, or even know his or her name, to all of a sudden be emotionally attached to making our point, to defending our self, or to getting him or her to do something we think he or she should do. And often we can't seem to let go of these thoughts and feelings. Our focus narrows and our blood pressure rises.

This book is about ideas on how to stop this self-destructive process of entanglement, how to retrieve our self when we are sliding into an interpersonal tangle or, worse yet, are already quite caught in its web. It describes a process for people who want to break free emotionally from relationships that are unhealthy for them. The roots of this process are based on what we have learned about people living with addiction, and I will be mentioning this relationship with addiction, one manifestation of which is alcoholism, throughout the book.

The issues that are present in relationships in which there is addiction are, however, often the same for those living in other unhealthy relationships, whether addiction is an overt factor or not. This includes people who

* are dealing with codependency;
* are adult children of people with addiction;
* love too much;
* are being emotionally or physically hurt in their relationships;
* want to fix others;
* want to get out of a relationship and can't;
* feel they have to be in full control of everything;
* take care of others more than themselves;
* mold themselves according to how they think others want them to be;
* focus more on the external than the internal;
* are unable to say "no."

The evolution of this book is itself a product of my own work to disentangle. It has developed as I have. What I write of in this book comes from my personal history and from my work as a psychotherapist. My personal journey brought me to these issues first, and the substance of this book would be sorely impoverished and somewhat dishonest if I did not share that history first.

"They care about me so much. I hate to disappoint them."

# 2 The First Twenty-or-So Years

In 1964 I was in the seventh grade. I remember liking two boys who were the troublemakers of the class. They were cute and funny. They would call me at home at night, and we would hang on the telephone for hours, not saying much. I was so glad they would call. I was charmed by their rebelliousness and lack of caring about their behavior. I never got in trouble with them. They never asked me to. I just vicariously enjoyed their "wildness" while I made straight As and held class offices.

By the summer before my ninth-grade year, I started dating a guy whom I would marry eight years later after I graduated from college. We dated all those years. On a few occasions we broke up briefly. During those times, I went out with the notorious school troublemaker who showed little to no respect for me and whose attention I deeply desired. His values had seemingly little to do with mine; his life goals seemed to be headed in a much different direction than mine. He was frequently drinking or under the influence. Neither my family nor I drank alcohol at all, but I sure liked this guy and made decisions to please him that still come to my mind in a troubling way.

The young man whom I dated for eight years and subsequently married was very devoted to me. He worked hard and gave me nice things. For many years it was "safe" for me to be with this person. My family loved him, as did my high school and college friends. He was a very sociable guy with a good sense of humor. By dating him, I did not have to deal with the multitude of decisions, rejections, and disappointments of dating other people. I did not have to think about me, about my values, my identity, my beliefs. I was able to mindlessly be in a relationship that was respectable and pleasing. I thought I was happy.

I thought I was happy until my senior year in college.

It was the spring of that year, 1974. I was to marry in May and graduate with my class shortly thereafter. I was doing it right by the book. My college friends were to be in my wedding. By the end of June I would have a degree and a husband, and return to live in the city in which I grew up.

My husband-to-be and I were at a sorority dance that spring. Somewhere, somehow, it came to me that night that I really did not want to go through with this wedding. Over the course of the evening I tried to explain this to my fiancé, and, by the end of the night, I had returned my engagement ring. Some part of me was aware that going this route of marriage now just didn't feel right.

Within a day of my breaking off the engagement, my family and friends were asking to talk with me about what was happening. The details of those conversations escape me still, even my feelings at that time. The end result of those conversations, however, I do recall: I changed my mind and decided to reinstate the engagement and proceed with the wedding as planned.

And so we were married in May, and I graduated in June. We lived in the city where I grew up, and I entered graduate school there.

Now to be clear, this story is about me. It is not about what other people did to me or my life. Granted, my life has been influenced by my relationships with others. However, here and now I am describing my fledgling self, a self that was just starting to be heard by me and was trying to speak up. But I was not really aware of this, and so I only experienced much of this as a big mess that I made and I needed to clean up.

We were married two years. My husband remained the fun-loving, generally attentive guy I had dated, and he offered comfort and companionship. I believe, however, that I was just not comfortable with the idea of being married. I was in graduate school during those years and worked in a psychiatric hospital. We lived in a townhouse in an urban area and had some fun decorating it and making it home. But I did not feel quite right with things.

My doubts about being married remained and grew. Over time I saw that there were important differences in the way my husband and I liked to spend time, in the company we would keep, and in some of our values. We decided to end our marriage.

I had no idea then that I was working on finding my self. Looking back on it now, I can see that a voice in me that hardly knew any words wanted me to know that I could not simply keep following external expectations, whether they were real or imagined by me. I was mindlessly living my life.

I had no idea I was mindless. If you had asked me, I would have thought I was rather focused and purposeful. I had always been a successful student, worker, and daughter. I tried very hard to please many people and seemed to succeed at that. I was rarely "in trouble."

My life looked pretty good, and in many ways felt pretty good, as I reaped benefits from my successes. But inside me, things were feeling confused and unsettled. I needed to do something different.

So I finished my master's degree and moved to the Shenandoah Valley, about three hours away from my childhood home. A new job took me in this direction. I was aware that I wanted to get out of the city and into the country. What I wasn't aware of then was that I also wanted to get some physical space for my self.

It wasn't until this time in my twenties that I realized how much I was influenced by my desire to please others. I cared so much about keeping my parents, my teachers, my friends happy with me. I feared their disapproval and their anger. I hated having anyone mad with me. It meant feelings of being bad and wrong. So I almost always tried to be good and to do things "right."

"Right" meant doing things according to the books, according to spoken and unspoken shoulds. "Right" meant "Do as I say." Certainly "right" also means doing things that are moral and ethical, and I am comfortable with that. It's just that my actions, my decisions, my behaviors were governed by watching those people whom I was trying to please and selecting a response or course of action that seemed to be what *they* wanted. And I mean I literally watched. I watched their faces and their behaviors for clues about how I thought they were feeling toward me.

I can still watch people. Even now, if I am feeling anxious and worried in my relationships with certain people, I will regress to my watching behavior. I look outside of my self and to others. I watch what their faces are showing me and listen carefully to clues in their speech or behaviors that tell me if they are disapproving or mad with me. I wonder what they are thinking and feeling. I want to know what they want from me, what would please them, what would make them happy, what would keep them from being angry with me.

To begin my escape from this pattern, I came to live in the Valley. I was moved to this action by a small, internal voice/ feeling that said this would be something I would like to do. And I was blessed by my ability to do so.

One of the good things about this rather random move was that it put me in a community in which I have been very happy. When I moved here, I told my self that this would be for at least two years. Two years have turned into thirty-three. This is now home to me.

Another good thing about this move was that I met the man who was to become my second husband and to whom I am still married. Through my years in a twelve-step program of recovery for the family members and significant others of people who suffer from addiction, I have come to understand what people mean when they say, "I'm glad I'm married to an alcoholic." They mean that this brought them into the program that has transformed their lives. The program has brought them to a level of peace and acceptance that they never knew possible. The program has helped them to focus on their own lives and to greatly enhance their spirituality. In this same way, I say it is good that I moved out here and met my husband, for my relationship with him led me to yet greater depths of "lostness in the other" and, subsequently, to finding my way out.

"Are you mad at me?"

# 3 The Second Twenty-or-So Years

*"If only I knew what he wanted from me."*

For the first eleven years of my life here in the Valley, I frolicked in my insanity unknowingly. By day I worked as the psychotherapist-of-delinquents. By night I took ballet classes, danced with a small dance company, and acted in summer stock theater. I fixed up my home, socialized with new friends, and enjoyed my cats. In many ways the times were good and just what I needed for autonomy and identity development. Granted, we know of those tasks as belonging to the adolescent phase of development. But there is no doubt in my mind that I did not really work on those developmental tasks until I was in my twenties. Prior to then I had appeared independent, but there was little independent thought and substance to me. I was driven by my needs to please others, to avoid conflict, and, as my work supervisor described me, to be "obsessively over-responsible."

In the context of Erik Erikson's stages of psychosocial development, as a result of having delayed the identity formation task of adolescence until my twenties, I was "behind" in my development related to the next stage—the cultivation of healthy intimate relationships. So during the first four or five years of living in the Valley, I dated some men and threw away one or two potentially good, loving relationships with seemingly stable men who cared about me. One in particular asked me to marry him, describing a lovely, festive wedding in our quaint community. This was more than I could bear. So I left him for another. I can only imagine that he must have wondered what the hell was wrong with me. It has taken me a long time to find out.

The man I left him for was the man who became my second husband. And this has been the most challenging relationship of all for me. I felt off-balance almost from the start. I was instantly attracted to him the first time I met him. He came into the building that housed my work office inquiring where he was to go to work for the evening shift. He was a new, temporary employee. I gave him the information he requested, and he went on his way. I wondered who he was and where he came from.

Within a short period of time, I gathered that information and started to get to know him through mutual friends. I learned bits here and there about him. The facts revealed that he had temporarily come to this area to live with a friend who had also recently moved here; he had previously lived in Cambridge, Massachusetts, in a commune; he had worked in a psychiatric hospital in Boston; he was thirty-seven years old and had held twenty-five jobs; he liked to have a six-pack of cheap beer at the end of every day.

And to these facts I added all sorts of bits and pieces of my own about who I *thought* he was. I thought he was a charming intellectual of New England descent. I thought he was brilliant, worldly, and sophisticated. I was fascinated by him. I thought he had fabulous ideas that put mine to shame. I thought he was deep. I thought he was exotic. I thought I was simple and plain and unexciting. I thought he was wonderful and I was not. I thought he could not possibly like me for who I was.

And so I became very attached to these illusions and to my desire to have him like me nevertheless. And so I created a sort of hell for my self that went on for years.

Recently, my husband and I were reviewing the names of the presidents of the United States in the twentieth century in response to some question by our daughter. My husband had the encyclopedia in his hands, and I was trying to recall them in order. When I thought I had successfully finished the list, my husband said, "That was all right except that you forgot Ronald Reagan. He was president for the first eight years of our relationship." He paused, and with a knowing smile he said, "I guess you missed that one because you thought I was president then." We laughed. I knew exactly what he meant.

The insecurities and self-doubts I put my self through during the first years of our relationship were awful. I remember consciously asking my self, "Would he like me if I looked like that?" "Would he think I was more interesting if I was like her?" I was constantly searching for what I could do to be appealing and interesting to him. I was sure I was not.

And small fights with him would devastate me. I would go off sobbing by my self and feel very lost and fearful that our relationship was certainly over.

I was always sure he would leave me.

I got to feeling so bad and off-center. I would feel like the bottom was dropping out from under me. I would feel agitated and unable to concentrate. Things that generally brought me pleasure were unimportant and cast aside. I would pursue arguments for hours, hoping that we could come to some point where I again would feel sure he was not going away. I would feel compelled to say some things to him and to seek his reassurance. As I approached such conversations, I would know that they would likely not produce the results I desired. But I pursued them anyway, wanting to hold onto this man.

And about "this man": This book is about me and will remain so. But it is important to make a few general comments about him that enrich this picture. This man did not shower me with gifts or verbalizations offering me the reassurance I sought. He had his own issues with work and intimacy and, as I've already hinted, alcohol. I had finally found the rebellious sort I sought out in the seventh grade. But this one was cloaked in intellect and social class that made our being together seem more appropriate and okay. He seemed hardly emotionally available to me, and this drew me in like a magnet.

And he knew this.

So it should have not been a surprise to me several years into our relationship when we were walking by a bookstore in a mall that he pointed out Robin Norwood's book *Women Who Love Too Much* to me. How insulting! How insightful! How correct!

This is how I handled the situation: A big part of me wanted to please him. So of course I showed interest in the book and the topic. I even bought it on the spot. A small part of me was bothered that he would even suggest that something was wrong with me, needless to mention with our relationship. And an even smaller part of me thought perhaps the help I knew I needed was to be had in that book.

And, in fact, it was. It was the beginning of the way out at last, the way out of my lostness, anxiety, and despair. A year or so prior to this I had entered psychotherapy to help me with these same issues. I had been feeling so bad in the relationship that I had seen a psychologist for the first time in my life. I had also done this because I thought my husband would like me to do it. He did.

The psychotherapy had been pleasant, comforting, and somewhat revealing, but our work had not really helped me with my entanglements with my husband. I don't think I shared the depths of those issues with this male psychotherapist. I was too ashamed, in part. I had an image of competence and togetherness to maintain. After all, I was a psychotherapist too, so I should know better. I should have it all together. It didn't help either that my therapist moved to another state before we finished our work. Nor did it help that the presence of alcoholism was never raised. So, insight I had gained, but my pain remained.

This was somewhere around 1985 or 1986. I started to get a clue that the way out of my entanglements involved getting my focus on my self and not on the other. But this was only a clue. Years of learning to disentangle were ahead of me.

Somewhere around this time I made a decision that was both healthy and unhealthy. For some reason I decided to apply to return to graduate school to complete my Ph.D. To my surprise, I was accepted into the program I sought. I was stunned and on the spot. I had not really thought about what I would do if I was accepted. To be in the program required moving to another part of the state. I waited until the very last day to give them my answer. And that answer was "No, thank you."

I declined this wonderful opportunity for two reasons. The healthy reason, or so it seemed to me, was that I was good at school and lousy at relationships. So I decided that rather than run away from this relationship, I would stay and work on it and me.

The other reason was the unhealthy one: I feared that if I went away to graduate school I would lose this man. I was sure of this and could not bear the thought of it happening. It felt like a great risk that my abandonment fears could not tolerate. So I said, "No, thank you."

I have not regretted that decision. I have in fact stuck with the course I picked at that time, which was to work on my intimacy difficulties and to increase my capacity for a healthy relationship. Consider this book my dissertation. It is the document that captures my experience, strength, and hope gathered through this educational path I chose in the mid-1980s.

In September 1987 we were married in a service on the front lawn of our home with our friends and my family present. In August 1988 our most wonderful daughter was born. In November 1988 my husband entered treatment. His diagnosis: alcoholism.

Finally, we had a name, a label, a way to conceptualize the craziness we had been living with. And we both took it seriously and embarked on our paths to recovery.

That was 1988. I started attending Al-Anon meetings almost right away, though not for particularly the right reasons. I saw the meetings as interesting and fun. I enjoyed hearing people's stories and intellectually absorbing the steps and traditions of the program. But I did not bring my emotional pain with me for a while. I had lost touch with it temporarily. My husband's diagnosis and treatment had given me some relief by showing that at least not all of this awfulness had been on me. That was good to know. But for a while, I lost touch with my insanity. Now that I knew he had been insane, I felt quite sane.

Thank heavens I continued to go to my meetings, because it wasn't long before my insanity was back. In my periodic journal I wrote:

> "I feel depressed . . . a feeling of dread . . . a feeling that I have been/am doing something very wrong."

> "I am consumed by my disease. I am anxious and depressed and my thinking is obsessive. . . . I am trying to lay low and hang with my higher power. Every which way I turn my thoughts are catastrophic."

My husband's being in recovery was vital, but it did not cure my insecurities, abandonment fears, or anxieties. It did not result in excellent communication between us, in improvement in our ability to work together, or in comfort with intimacy. All of those energy-sapping difficulties were still there. And this time we each had identified people and resources we could use to help us. My twelve-step program became a major influence for me.

In one of my twelve-step meetings a member said, "My therapist does not like for me to come to these meetings. He says they brainwash you. But you know, I think my brain needed washing." Yes, my brain needed washing as well. The ways I thought about my self and relationships and how to get what I thought I wanted all needed remaking. I needed to learn to think about me and not the other so much. I needed to learn when I was forcing solutions and to stop this. I needed to learn what I could and could not control. I needed to learn that insanity was continuing to do the same thing and expecting different results. I needed to cultivate my spirituality. And the rethinking goes on and on.

In fact, the body of this book describes in detail what I have learned from this program and from my experiences as I have tried to apply this program, as Step Twelve suggests, "in all my affairs." I have been on this path for twenty-two years. I have had the help of many excellent members from my twelve-step fellowship, an incredible sponsor, and several good and knowing friends outside the program. They have offered me inspiring thoughts that have helped to guide me to new places:

*"One person drinks and
the rest of us go crazy."*

*"I abandon my self."*

*"Our thinking becomes distorted by
trying to force solutions."*

*"What I need to know will come to my
attention without any effort on my part."*

*"We keep the focus on ourselves
and not the alcoholic."*

*"The evidence that my higher power
is going before me is so strong."*

I also had the wonderful help of a therapist and mentor who has a deep and experienced understanding of these issues of losing your self to another. She offered me insight after insight about my self and ways to find and keep my self. My journal is full of concise, to-the-point statements she offered me to help with this rethinking:

*"You have not succeeded in pleasing him so far.*
*You are not going to please him. So please you."*

*"Just act like a person would.*
*You don't have to get permission."*

*"Find the truth in whatever ways you can."*

*"Letting go is scary as hell because*
*it involves a leap of faith."*

And I have learned so much by my work with my clients. It was their questions to me about how to handle some of these same feelings and issues that pushed me to think through the details of this work even more thoroughly and methodically and to in fact create the first draft of what is now this book.

"I felt like I gave my self away."

# 4 Others on This Journey

*The following people are fictionalized characters based on real clients with whom I have worked. The real clients are aware that they have been fictionalized and have read and approved the characters based on them. This fictionalization is intended not only to protect the confidentiality of the clients but also to protect the confidentiality of others in their stories. The essence of their issues remains accurate and clear.*

## Elizabeth

It is 1992. I'm working in my private practice office with Elizabeth. She is a beautiful woman of fifty-five years. She holds a doctorate degree in social work and is the director of a social services agency serving a relatively large region in our area. She is highly respected for her competence, sincerity, and reliability. She is articulate and bright and very sad. She has come to me for relationship problems. On this particular day in November we are talking about her relationship with her husband of thirty years.

Elizabeth describes a deteriorating relationship with her husband for the last five years and even more so over the last two years. "Nothing I say is right." "I never know how he's going to react." "He needs to defy me, to fight with me." "I feel attacked."

I have inquired about his alcohol use. She reports some incidents of abuse of alcohol but is unclear about whether there is enough evidence of alcoholism.

Elizabeth is today particularly hooked by wanting to help her husband solve his problems. She is a very good problem-solver. Resourceful and creative, Elizabeth often uses these talents in constructive and desirable ways in her personal and professional life. But in her relationship with her husband, this just isn't working out so well.

Elizabeth says that her husband comes to her complaining about problems with his real estate business. She listens and then tries to offer what might "fix" this situation. She believes that he has come to her for this. But no. When she tries to "help," he rejects her offerings in a wide assortment of ways, all of which lead to conflict between them that sometimes gets mean, loud, and hurtful. They have been hurt, saddened, and lost by this repeating cycle of entanglement.

Today we are looking at ways to break that cycle, things Elizabeth could do differently to interrupt this deadly pattern. Yes, deadly. Though Elizabeth is not suicidal, she is quite despondent and discouraged. And though she says she would not kill her self, she does have thoughts of wishing she was dead. We know that untreated addiction can result in death or insanity. We need to acknowledge that untreated entanglements can result in the same tragic ends.

So we start to talk about emotionally backing off when these "help me / don't help me" arguments start. We start to talk about listening and detachment. Elizabeth says to me, "Detachment is very hard for me. . . . How would you do that?"

How would you do that? How do you detach? I am struck by this basic question. I know some answers to it, thankfully, because I have been doing my own work in and out of my twelve-step program. It is both an easy and a difficult question to answer. I know that Al-Anon has given me some excellent ideas of what detachment is and when to do it. So have some of the books I have read, especially *Women Who Love Too Much* and *Codependent No More*. I know that some basic healthy communication skills also facilitate this process of detachment. I also realize that I have cultivated some of my own internal techniques for detaching as I have been working on these issues for my self. And I know how hard it is to detach even if you know ways to do it. It is very hard.

I respond to Elizabeth by verbally offering a list of ideas of ways to detach. This list is coming off the top of my head and is drawing off the resources I just described. I jot this list down very roughly as I say it. I have never put these ideas together in this concrete, pragmatic way before. The information has been developing there for a while, and I have been testing it out, but I have never laid it out for me or someone else in this way.

This feels like a good thing to be doing.

And before my work day is over, I find my self offering this list again and again, enriching it each time. Client after client asks me questions about detachment and similar emotional entanglements that have brought them to therapy. Their stories are each quite unique. Their entanglements involve different relationships. Addiction may clearly be present, or it may not be. Clients may identify them selves as adult children of people with addictions or as abused, or they may not. The way they identify themselves is not nearly as important as is their experience of losing their self in and to another person.

## Anne

A few hours later, Anne comes for her appointment. She is in her late twenties, a small woman with sandy brown hair cut short and framing her face. She dresses quite fashionably and is eager to talk. She often has a smile on her face, but an edge of anger runs through much of what she has to say. We have been working together for a good while. Anne first came to see me shortly after she married. She was feeling so upset, confused, and depressed then about the angry and insecure way she felt around her husband. "He pisses me off" is a common sentence to hear from Anne.

Today Anne is focusing on her bad feelings about an important job from which she has been recently released. Anne had been working as the manager for a popular women's clothing store. She had been very excited about this opportunity for career growth and had taken her work seriously. She had expressed concern to me, but she was not clear about all she was supposed to do and how to do it. She had described feeling overwhelmed at the store at times and feared that her boss was not satisfied with her work. Indeed, today she tells me her fears have come true, and she has been released from the store's employment completely. She talks about wishing she had more supervision and feedback before they made their decision to ask her to leave. She is feeling angry and oh-so-bad about her self. Her feelings of failure and worthlessness are dominant. She easily recalls messages from her parents that told her that she could not make it on her own, that she should find a husband to support her and become a housewife. She is thinking this may be right after all.

Anne is asking, "Is it me? Was I wrong?" This is also a common sentence to hear from Anne. She has asked this many times as she has sorted through the issues with her husband. It is so easy for her to think it is *all* her problem. It is so easy for her to believe that everything would be fine if it wasn't for her.

Now this is a good question to ask our self: "What part do I play in this problem?" And I believe we do need to do this. The problem here is that Anne, like many of us, takes on the majority, if not all, of the responsibility for the problem, whatever it may be. In so doing, we bog our self down completely with guilt, defeat, and hopelessness, which equals depression, so that we can hardly function, much less find our way out of the problem. We are lost to the totality of our self. We see only the dark and inadequate. We exaggerate the dark and inadequate. And we believe that is all there is of us.

Today Anne has lost her self to the store and to her boss with whom she worked. As Anne says, she's feeling "lousy." This situation is the singular focus of her thoughts and feelings both in and out of this office.

## Charlotte

As Anne leaves, Charlotte arrives. Charlotte is in her thirties. Her shoulder-length hair bounces as she comes in, and she greets me with friendly, sparkling eyes. She is a jolly sort. She smiles and jokes a lot. She makes both of us laugh. Charlotte and I agree that Sharon Wegscheider-Cruse must have had her in mind when she wrote the description for the Mascot role in alcoholic families in her book *Another Chance: Hope and Health for the Alcoholic Family*. Indeed, Charlotte comes from a large, alcoholic family. Charlotte's father was an untreated alcoholic who committed suicide two years ago. Charlotte worked as a flight attendant until several years ago when she married. She now lives with her husband and their two-year-old daughter and works part-time for a travel agency.

Charlotte is a relatively new client. She came to me several months ago concerned about her relationship with her husband and her tendency to spend too much money on stuff she does not need or really want. She thought perhaps she was "addicted to Wal-Mart."

I have learned that Charlotte's husband works many hours away from home at his job. He gets up early to go to work and returns in the early evening. Many evenings he spends working on their home and yard. When he sits down in a living room chair at the end of his day, he falls asleep. Charlotte wants to talk with him and hear from him about just anything. Often he has little to say. Charlotte struggles constantly with how to handle this relationship that she values and wishes to maintain.

Today, though, Charlotte is talking about her difficulties with her mother-in-law. She is feeling very angry with this woman who she believes wants Charlotte to say and do things the way she thinks they should be done. Charlotte both wants to please her and to tell her to get lost. On one side, Charlotte says, "I feel sorry for her." On the other side, she says, "She thinks I'm not supposed to go anywhere. . . . Well, I got her number: Her number is she wants to make me feel bad. . . . But I don't know what to do with it [i.e., her number]."

Then, in her characteristic way, Charlotte adds, "Isn't that terrible?"

"Isn't *what* terrible?" I ask her.

"Isn't it terrible that I feel this way about her?"

And then, also in a characteristic way, she adds, "What should I do? What should I say? Did I do the right thing with her on the phone the other night?"

## Mark

In the evening of this same November day, Mark comes for his appointment after a full day in his office. He is a handsome man in his forties. He has a professional business which he owns. Mark, too, has a clever sense of humor that comes with him as he deals with his deeply troubling issues.

Mark entered therapy after he was left by his wife of many years. That relationship had been happy and vibrant for Mark. They had good times and were carefully planning for their future together. With seemingly little notice, she ended the relationship and quickly got involved with someone else, and today Mark has come in telling me that he has just learned that she is now engaged to the guy and plans to be married as soon as their divorce is finalized.

Mark has already been using therapy time to look at his high tolerance for the emotional instability that was also characteristic of their relationship. "It's always been a roller coaster . . . always something going on." He has also been looking at his obsession with her that has come out in thoughts and in writings he has done. He has been obsessed with trying to understand her and to get some answers from her.

Now he is starting to feel obsessed with his anger toward her as well. In talking about her recent engagement, he says, "That makes me mad. . . . I feel anger and disdain."

In a healthy effort to save his self, Mark adds, "I have to remember it's crazy. . . . I don't need to be in a relationship with anyone who would do what she has done."

* * * * *

Meanwhile, in my therapy work with college students, clients with similar experiences were presenting themselves. The following two young women came in for counseling around this same time. And my work with them was an essential part of the development of these ideas for disentangling. Several days after I saw Elizabeth, Anne, Charlotte, and Mark, I saw these students for therapy.

# Lindsey

Lindsey is a nineteen-year-old college junior with beautiful blonde hair and a long, tall figure. She has excellent grades and a full scholarship to college. She told me in her intake session that she has a history of bulimia, for which she was hospitalized in high school. She is not bulimic now, but does have a tendency to over-exercise. She also tends toward obsessive thinking. She seems to have a lot of insight and motivation to work in therapy.

When she first came to see me several weeks ago, she explained that she was feeling "really unfocused . . . pulled in all directions." Fairly quickly on the heels of this she told me, "This summer I realized that my mother is alcoholic." Her mother denies that she has a problem with alcohol. Her mother is divorced from Lindsey's father and lives on her own. Her mother can be emotional and dependent on Lindsey for advice and support. She can also be very critical of Lindsey.

Today Lindsey is feeling a lot of confusion about how to handle this relationship with her mother, even though it is long-distance. Breaks from college find her spending her time at home with her mother. Financially, she is still dependent on her as well. And at a more basic level, Lindsey would simply like to have a good relationship with her mother.

She is quite torn and confused. Like Charlotte, Lindsey is pulled in different directions. On one hand, she wants very much to help her mother in whatever ways are needed. She wants very much for her mother to be happy, saying, "If she was happy, I'd be happier." On the other hand, Lindsey says, "She's crazy, and she makes me feel like I'm crazy." Lindsey states that her mother's negative views about things "rub off on me."

No wonder that Lindsey feels "pulled in all directions."

Her personal goals include becoming more *self*-aware and less confused without feeling like she's "abandoning my family."

## Trish

Later in the afternoon on this same day, Trish comes for her fifth appointment with me. Trish is an eighteen-year-old college freshman. She is a petite young woman with short, bouncy hair.

She has a sweet smile and a very tentative way of speaking and presenting her self. She acknowledges being shy and having a history of being picked on and teased.

Trish entered therapy because of adjustment problems to college life. She described feeling both anxious and depressed since starting college. In our initial session, she described having trouble breathing at times and feeling "so dark inside." Many of her issues seemed to focus around peer relationships. She described her self as worrying a great deal about the question "Do people like me?" She said she had this problem in high school, but it had gotten better. "This insecurity thing came back when I got to college. . . . I'm afraid that if people really know me, they won't like me."

As part of her history, Trish has told me about a difficult relationship with her father. Trish's mother and father divorced when she was eleven, and she has had regular visitation with her father. She describes him as demanding and controlling. Trish has tried for years to feel like she is pleasing him but believes she is "never good enough." Trish has said to me that she still hopes that "maybe I'll get him to really like me."

Today, however, Trish wants to talk about her attachment to a peer on her campus, an attachment that is making her feel obsessed and frustrated. Trish describes an intense interest in this person who lives near her. The person parties a lot, studies very little, and comes to Trish's room to borrow her things. Trish is aware that this is a "bad relationship" for her in that it leaves her feeling inadequate and not okay. She states that she tries hard to "conform" to what she thinks this other person wants her to be. She states, "I'm hooked. . . . I have no life outside of her." Trish is aware of all of these thoughts and feelings but expresses an inability to do anything different.

Her healthy self states that one of her therapy goals is to find her own identity, to be able to say, "This is me, and I'm okay with me."

* * * * *

And then there are also teenagers working on these same issues in counseling. Many have surfaced over the years in my private practice work, but one case in particular has been with me through the development of this disentangling work and is rich in details of lostness and growth.

# Rebecca

Rebecca is a sixteen-year-old sophomore in high school. She is a pretty, petite young woman who is bright and articulate. We have been working together for two years. Rebecca first came to see me after being raped by an acquaintance while on a beach vacation with her parents. She was very depressed and convinced that "it was all my fault." She was being "harsh" on her self about what happened to her. She was tearful, moody, and having some flashbacks from the rape. Just prior to our first appointment, she made a suicidal gesture of cutting on her wrist with a razor. I facilitated her hospitalization, which stabilized her in a matter of days, and she returned to our community and began her therapy work with me.

Rebecca's work over these two years has helped her greatly with exploring and starting to form her identity. She has become more stable in her moods and more accepting of her self. She continues to work on relationships, particularly intimacy. She knows she has a tendency to jump in with both feet really fast, and in so doing scares others away. She can be too open, allowing her self to be vulnerable often to the wrong people. She has come to know that she can too easily "self-sabotage."

And she often describes her self as "an extremist," meaning that she goes from one extreme to the other, and that she is all-or-nothing no matter what the situation or relationship may be. "Extreme in everything I do," she says. "My grades have to be perfect, and everything has to be up to my standards of everything-is-under-control. I can't stand to not be understood or for there to be a problem. I have to solve things immediately."

Today Rebecca is struggling with the ending of her relationship with her first real boyfriend. She has been with Ben for a year and a half. The relationship has been relatively stable and supportive, tender, and kind. This fall, however, Ben moved with his family to their new home about four hours away. After one month there, his relationship with Rebecca began to fall apart as their lives took different directions. Over the month of November, they have been struggling with what to do with their relationship now. Ben has expressed his wanting to end it; Rebecca wants to keep it.

Today Rebecca tells me she has received a letter from Ben saying, "I've fallen out of love with you. . . . Give me some space."

Rebecca is distraught. "He never loved me. I'm absolutely baffled with life. I haven't even grasped it. It hurts like a bitch!"

She is depressed and consumed with this problem. "I missed the PSATs on Saturday because I was arguing with him. I've missed lots of classes and am behind on my work. And I don't want to get high, but I'm weak now and probably will."

And she goes further: "I can't deal with this. I feel like I have no control. I never realized how obsessive I am. My thoughts always drift to 'it's not worth it.' I get in these fits. If I had sleeping pills, I would be dead.

"This whole thing with Ben is driving me crazy. I want him in my life."

It's just good common sense.

In a way I'm glad I'm out of there.

I can stay in
my marriage
and be my self.

# untangling

(as shared by various people along the way)

Unbelievable I have

been so wrapped up

in one individual.

I feel like I'm coming
out of the twilight zone.

"It's just good common sense."

# 5 The Big Picture

The problem was clearly laid out before me. I had experienced entanglements for years, and now some important pieces of how to untangle my self were all starting to come together. I had been gathering them for my self in random ways, but my work with my clients pushed me to get down to some of the nuts and bolts of "how to," to pull together these important pieces in a way that would increase all of our chances of finding our self again and of increasing peace and serenity in our lives.

The themes of entanglement issues were clear:

*What is wrong with me?*

*Am I doing something wrong?*

*Who am I separate from this other person?*

*Do I know who I am?*

*Do I know what I think?*
*feel? know? believe? want?*

*Can I survive having more emotional*
*distance from this other person?*

*If I back off, will he or she leave me?*

*If I back off, will he or she survive?*

*If I back off, will I survive?*

*How much of the problem is me?*

*What should I do about his or her problem?*

*What should I do about my problem?*

*How much do I want to put up with?*

*What do I do when I've had enough?*

*Suppose I don't know if I've had enough?*

*What do you mean, "What do I want?"*

*What do you mean, "What's good for me?"*

And so I wrote a draft of ideas on how to disentangle. I compiled ideas from the many areas that had influenced me and taught me over the last ten years. I added in ideas drawn from my own experience, strength, and hope. I wrote a draft, rewrote it, and rewrote it, adding, revising, editing. It is still a work in progress, always organic, always subject to new ideas, always subject to revisions of the old. As I move along on this journey, I continue to see old things in new ways, to see how what I perceive and understand today may be altered by a new insight tomorrow.

Even though this list of ideas is subject to constant revision, it has also remained essentially the same at its core. Revisions allow increased depth in our work. The core list, entitled *Ideas on How to Disentangle*, reads as follows:

## Ideas on How to Disentangle

Our **illusions** keep us attached and entangled.

Facing our illusions, detaching, setting healthy boundaries, and developing our spirituality can help us to disentangle.

### Facing Illusions

∗ Find *the truth* about your situation.

∗ Work with your self to accept the truth you find.

### Detaching

∗ Become aware of who and what *entangles* you:

- Who do you get entangled with?
- What entangles you with them?
- What parts of you get entangled?
- How do you act and feel when you're entangled?

∗ Learn to separate out what is your problem and what is the other person's problem.

✳ Don't try to fix his or her problem.

✳ Work for some emotional distance:

    • *Observe* the other more than fully interact with him or her, as loss of your self is likely if you do get fully into the interaction.

    • Try to *act* out of your *centeredness* and not out of your *reactions* to the other person.

    • Use *self-talk* to help you when you are feeling pulled off your center (e.g., "I'm okay." "It's okay to say this." "I haven't done anything wrong." "This is not my issue.").

    • Be aware of the motivations behind what you say and do in interacting with the other. Make sure you are not saying or doing things to manipulate, control, or change them or to make them feel a certain way or do something specific. You are most likely to keep your centeredness if your motivation is to express your self assertively.

## Setting Healthy Boundaries

✳ Slow down.

✳ Listen to your own needs, wants, limits, beliefs, feelings.

✳ Make "I" statements rather than ask questions.

✳ Set and state your boundaries.

✳ Mean your limits and stick with them.

✳ Say things once.

✳ Say things cleanly and without extensive discussion.

✳ Stick to the topic.

✳ Stay in the present.

* Listen to the other person.

* Acknowledge you hear what the other is saying, but try not to defend, rationalize, explain, justify, or convince in response to him or her. By doing so, you can lose your centeredness.

* Be aware and observe your emotions and behaviors as you express those emotions and behaviors.

* Learn when to stop.

* Stop.

## Developing Spirituality

* Slow down.

* Simplify.

* Be in the present.

* Find some solitude.

* Breathe deeply.

* Relax your body.

* Quiet your mind.

* Sit in silence.

* Discover your higher power.

* Have an ongoing relationship with your higher power.

* Let go of things you cannot control.

* Practice these things.

* Cultivate faith.

*Compiled by Nancy L. Johnston*

This list takes a look at the big picture of disentangling. It is an overview of ideas that collectively give us power and confidence and serenity and hope for our self. I offer this to clients in individual and/or group therapy. I do not routinely offer it to clients until, as I get to know them, I see the value in their working on these elements. I am amazed at how often I do share this information. Certainly, clients coming in for help with family members and friends suffering from addiction frequently benefit by work in this area. Other clients are less clear in needing this information at first.

A client of mine came in for panic attacks and anxiety. The panic was interfering with his daily functioning, making him miss his construction work for fear that he would have an attack. He had ulcers and periodic rashes. As I got to know him, he talked about his concerns about his relationship with his wife, who had several affairs. She did not want to commit to him and did not want to leave, either. It quickly became clear how entangled he was in their relationship and absolutely stuck about what to do next.

A woman came to see me, concerned about her anger toward her young children and wanting to learn how to manage her feelings and behaviors with them. I learned about her history of a harsh and controlling childhood with her grandparents by whom she was raised. Her anger level at her grandfather was still very strong. She readily reexperienced his teasing, criticism, and sexual harassment of her. She was furious with him. She was angry with her children, one of whom reminded her of her grandfather. She could hardly contain her self.

So, person by person, as I see the need, I pull out my handout, I copy it again, and we start to work on the pieces of disentangling, weaving together the influences of psychology, self-help, philosophy, and experience.

And as I have worked with these individuals, sometimes one right after the other, I have been struck by how similar their issues and feelings are despite the differences in the content and details of their stories. And so, I have formed Disentangle Groups, where these people come together and talk to each other. They can share their stories and feelings. They can break their feelings of isolation. And they can gather skills, insight, and life.

The advertisement for our groups summarizes much of what disentangling is all about, whether the person is doing that work individually or with a group:

# DISENTANGLE

## A COUNSELING GROUP

**For people who are want to break free emotionally from relationships that are unhealthy for them. This would include people who:**

• are dealing with codependency;

• are adult children of people with addictions;

• love too much;

• are being emotionally or physically hurt in their love relationships;

• want to get out of a relationship and can't;

• feel they have to be in full control of everything;

• take care of others more than themselves.

*These relationships may be with anyone—parents, friends, romantic partners, children, co-workers, bosses, etc.*

• • • • •

The theoretical roots of this group are based on what we have learned about people living with addiction, and the same issues are present for many living in other unhealthy relationships. Thus, **the group is open to anyone who feels too entangled with other(s).**

**The group intends to help members set boundaries for themselves that will enable them to disentangle from others and feel better.**

The following chapters will take this overview of disentangling and look at the pieces of it in more detail, pieces that have become clearer and more describable as we have worked and lived with these ideas.

First we will look at what I call *The Basics*. *The Basics* are general descriptions of what disentangling is about. *The Basics* are intended to help you understand what this process involves and what it can offer you.

Then we will explore *The Four Areas of Work* involved in disentangling, looking at each of the *Ideas on How to Disentangle* previously presented. We will look at what each idea means, reasons for its usefulness, and practical ways to apply it.

"Now what what do you mean by 'Disentangle'?"

*Charlotte, age 34*

# 6 The Basics

In this chapter we will be looking at some general concepts that describe the process of disentangling. Before a person embarks on this path of self-retrieval, I believe it is important for him or her to understand not only some "how-tos" of the process, but also some general guidelines about how it works and what to expect and not to expect.

Clients coming to psychotherapy for the first time need education from us about the therapy process. They have no idea what to expect. Sometimes I have found that without some information from me, they expect it to be somewhat like seeing a medical doctor, where they describe their symptoms and the doctor writes a prescription that may take care of the problem with one visit. Clients often ask questions about how long the therapy may take and whether their therapy work will help them to help or change another person in their life. They are unfamiliar with our ethics of confidentiality, sanctions against dual relationships, and the professional boundaries we employ with these people who sometimes want us to also be their friend. They need my professional guidance on these process issues.

Similarly, the process of disentangling merits an explanation. It can be described in terms of what it is and is not about. I have developed this description over the years as I have introduced and explained to people what I mean by disentangling.

Some people immediately find the word "disentangle" to be a good one. The expression on their face and the glimmer in their eyes tells me that they know what entanglement is, and they just might see and desire untangling from something or somebody. It hits a familiar chord.

It is not uncommon for people who are attached to something or somebody to experience anxiety and skepticism when I mention this word and process. Their abandonment issues immediately come to the surface. They fear I am talking about separation, about divorce, about being alone and empty forever.

Then there are those who think to disentangle would be selfish. What will happen to the other person if they don't take care of him or her? Wouldn't it be wrong to not help/take care of him or her? Guilt comes pouring forth, guilt at any thought of saying or doing things to take care of their self.

And then there is the reaction from the person who tells me she simply has no idea what I am talking about when I suggest that she take a look at her self first. *She* is not the one with the problem. She has come to me to get help for the other. She is confused and lost by the idea of disentangling, and may even feel put off, believing that I am not responding to the issues that brought her to therapy.

The following ten descriptions offer an explanation of what I mean when I talk about the process of disentangling. This information can help you to understand what this process is all about, what it can offer you, and what your part is in the process.

# It's About the Experience of Losing Your Self

Disentangling is about recognizing that you have lost your self in someone else. It is about the experience of being consumed with worry, care, thoughts, anxieties, plans, regrets, anger, frustration, confusion, exhilaration, anticipation, fantasies, hopes, and dreams about another person. It is about the experience of feeling lost and not knowing what to do next. It is about the experience of hardly being able to take care of what needs to be done. It is the experience of fear and dark expectations and impending doom. It is about the experience of a high that feels absolutely great and that you seek to feel again and again. It is about the experience of having little to no awareness of you and what you need. It is about the experience of not being aware that you are not in touch with you.

Disentangling is a process that is for people who identify themselves in a variety of ways. It is about the experience of losing your self to another person. I have found this experience to be common among people whether they identify themselves as codependent, as adult children of people with addiction, or as people who love too much. I discovered this as I put together and ran an assortment of therapy groups over the years. I ran an Adult Children of Alcoholics (ACOA) counseling group and a *Women Who Love Too Much* group. My clients in individual therapy often were working on codependency issues. As I worked with these populations somewhat separately, I realized that their issues were often similar, if not the same. I realized that though the specifics of their situations were different, they were each entangled with other people and sacrificing their self in the process.

Codependence has not yet achieved one agreed-upon definition. Codependents Anonymous (CoDA) suggests that people look at their control and compliance patterns in order to determine if they might benefit by their participation in CoDA.

In *Codependent No More,* Melody Beattie defines codependence thus: "A codependent person is one who has let another person's behavior affect him or her, and who is obsessed with controlling that person's behavior."[*]

Timmen L. Cermak, working with the clinical model of the *Diagnostic and Statistical Manual of Mental Disorders,* defines codependence as "a recognizable pattern of personality traits" that include "continued investment of self-esteem in the ability to influence/control feelings and behavior, both in oneself and in others, in the face of serious adverse consequences" and "assumption of responsibility for meeting others' needs, to the exclusion of acknowledging one's own needs."[*]

Robin Norwood's subtitle to *Women Who Love Too Much* is "When You Keep Wishing and Hoping He'll Change." She describes loving too much as a process that involves low self-esteem, a need to be needed, a strong urge to change and control others, and a willingness to suffer.

All of these definitions are useful to me and to my clients. They all address real people and real problems. I have found it helpful, though, to see that at the core of all of these definitions is the experience of the loss of self. And I have found that

---

[*] Reprinted by permission of Hazelden Foundation, Center City, MN.

clients find this a useful way to work with their problems. We do not have to decide if they are codependent or not. Some clients resist this description or what they think this description means. We don't have to get hung up on whether they self-diagnose in this way. Sometimes their entanglements do not involve controlling, compliance, or caretaking behaviors. We don't have to find the addiction in their family histories or people they are trying to change. We only have to get in touch with their experience of losing their self in another and the insanity that follows.

Entanglements are about losing your self in someone else. Your response to that entanglement may be quite varied. You may want to control the other, fix or change him or her. You may want to simply be with him or her no matter what. You may be willing to change your self so that you can be with him or her. Regardless of your response to the entanglement, the process of disentangling is about your lost self and how to retrieve you from that tangled mess.

THE BASICS

# It's About Unhealthy Attachments

It is normal to want things. It is normal to desire love and companionship. It is normal to get attached to things and people that mean a lot to you. It is normal to care about others and to wish them well. It is even normal to extend our self to other people or to causes we may take on. These are the things that can enrich our lives, give them increased depth and meaning, and help us to understand our self better. These are healthy attachments.

Disentangling is about attachments that have become unhealthy. The *Diagnostic and Statistical Manual of Mental Disorders (DSM)* is the principal reference for diagnosing mental health problems. One of the criteria the *DSM* uses for many of the disorders it covers is that the condition must cause significant distress or problems in important areas of life functioning, such as relationships, work, school, health, etc. I think this is a useful concept not only in defining the diagnosable clinical problems of my clients, but also in looking at this idea of unhealthy attachments.

Unhealthy attachments can cause significant impairment in social or occupational functioning. An unhealthy attachment to another person may cause us to:

* not go to work or to school;
* fail to be prepared for work or school;
* neglect our children;
* neglect our health;
* neglect our responsibilities;
* misspend our money;
* hide in bed all day or all week;
* contract a sexually transmitted disease;
* get arrested;
* lie;
* steal;
* cheat;
* lose our job;
* lose our temper;
* lose our friends;
* lose our family;
* lose our mind.

Unhealthy attachments lead us to losing track of what's important to us. They preoccupy our thoughts and then they can preoccupy our behaviors. We pursue, snoop, sneak, watch, and wait. And we wait and wait, waiting for things to be better, for things to be more like we'd like them to be. And the rest of our life goes to hell. And we don't even care. We may not even notice. It just doesn't seem to matter.

All that matters is this person to whom we have become attached. All that matters are our thoughts and behaviors that are riveted on this person and his or her thoughts and behaviors. Our focus has become so narrow that this is all we see. We have blinders on to the other parts of our life and, ironically, blinders on to the reality of our relationship with this other person. We are so up in his or her face that we cannot see clearly. We are so up in his or her face that our daily functioning with other people, with work, and with care of our self is shot. We have developed an unhealthy attachment.

THE BASICS

# It's About Finding You

The process of disentangling is about retrieving our self from the tangled web in which we have become caught. It's about removing the threads (or ropes) that have us bound to this unhealthy attachment. Then, once we have some freedom to move and think, it's about getting enough emotional distance from the situation so we can see it more clearly and make better decisions.

It is not necessarily a process about leaving someone else. This is not about desertion or divorce. Rather, this process is directed at helping you to either find your self, perhaps for the first time, or to get back the self you had but seem to have abandoned as you developed an unhealthy attachment.

Some of us have never really quite had a self, even though we may have looked just fine. For the majority of our lives, our decisions, behaviors, and language have been based more on what others might think of us or want us to do or be. We have had an extremely external focus that observes our environment and then dictates what we should say or do. And we have faithfully followed that external lead. We have in some ways been rewarded for this external focus. We have pleased others, minimized conflicts, and often been the ones to see that responsibilities got taken care of. We are seen as reliable and responsible. This has become an identity of ours.

There is nothing wrong with this identity in and of itself. The problem comes when that identity has been based almost entirely on external demands and expectations. The internal self has been neglected and is not known or can hardly be heard. Disentangling is a process that invites and fosters this focus on the internal self: What do *you* need, want, feel, believe, and/or think?

And then there are others who have cultivated a more balanced identity over the years, who have been aware of their self and who have been able to assert that self adequately. And then, without their awareness, they have begun to lose that self in their relationship with another person. Twelve-step literature describes the disease of addiction as cunning, baffling, and powerful. Well, our vulnerability to unhealthy attachments can also be cunning, baffling, and powerful. Without being aware, we can allow our self to be eroded for what we believe is the benefit of the relationship to which we are attached.

So, the ideas for disentangling are intended to help *you* get in touch with *you*. The process does not predict what will happen to your relationship as a result of your disentangling. Disentangling is not about playing an unhealthy game of backing off so the other person will come closer. It is not an unhealthy game about backing off so you can scare the other person into doing something that you want them to do. Disentangling is not intended to be used to manipulate others in any way. Disentangling is something you do for you to help you get your feet back on the ground, to help you become less confused, and to help you have more serenity in your life.

Your relationship may benefit by your disentangling in that it probably will interrupt the unhealthy patterns that have developed there. As you change and act differently in the relationship, it is just a natural law that others in the relationship will change also. By your changes, you are changing the sick balance of this relationship system.

We have no idea, however, how the other will change in response to your change. Change is hard for all of us. And you can expect that initially, your change will not be well received, and the other person may try hard, in a variety of ways, to get things back to how they used to be, even if things were sick. We may even retreat to the old patterns. We are attracted to the familiar. At least we each knew how to act and react when things were not so good. Now, as things may be changing, neither of us is as clear about what to say or do next.

Your disentangling does not guarantee that your relationship will improve or be ideal. Your disentangling does not guarantee that your relationship will end. Your disentangling does offer you the opportunity to find you. It offers you the opportunity to have some solid ground under your feet so that you don't feel blown by the winds of the relationship. It offers you the opportunity to get off the roller coaster you are on and to watch it for a while so you can decide what you want to do.

THE BASICS
# It's About Getting Balance

Many of us who are prone to entanglements are also prone to extremes. We believe we have to give *all* of our self *or none* of our self. We have to have all of someone's attention or we want nothing to do with him or her. We think we have to meet every request or need or he or she will be gone. Usually we opt for giving all of our self to the other. So, when I suggest to a person that we focus on his or her needs rather than the needs of another, it is not unusual for him or her to ask me, "Wouldn't that be selfish? I don't want to be selfish." He or she has immediately jumped in thinking from the extreme of losing him or her self in another to the extreme of complete selfishness. There *is* something in the middle.

We need to learn to live in the gray. We tend to see things as black or white, all or nothing. Living in the gray is a real challenge for those of us who are driven by our insecurities, by our demand to know what's going on right now, and what it all means. In the absence of solid information, we fill in the blanks with our own fears and worries. And then we jump to one of our great extremes of thought: "It's over." "He doesn't love me at all." "She never loved me." "I'll never be happy and loved in a relationship." "I'm not loveable at all." "I never was loveable anyway."

Finding a balance in our thoughts, feelings, and behaviors is an important part of disentangling. It may not be unhealthy for you to be in a particular relationship if you can strike a balance for your self between your focus on the other and your focus on your self. We don't necessarily have to end a relationship if we can find a point where our needs are equally considered and respected.

A client was talking to me about an upcoming week-long visit to the home of her mother for a holiday. Her mother was in active addiction and lived alone. My client was torn about how to handle this visit. She was feeling guilty because she had not visited her mother in a long time and was worried about her mother's drinking. On the other hand, my client was feeling disinclined to go. She knew how hard it was to be around her mother who was emotionally dependent on her and who overwhelmed her with her depression, fears, and anger. Should she go or not go?

"Perhaps there is something in the middle," I suggested. "You don't have to go for the entire week, nor do you have to not go at all. Perhaps you could do some of both."

"I never thought of that," she said.

That's right. We don't think of both. We think of either/or. We think things have to be this way or that. We think we have to give completely of our self or not at all.

My husband has been doing a great deal of thinking and writing about this concept of "both/and." He says that, for example, "politically, you have liberals talking community support and conservatives talking individualism, and you have to have both. . . . One without the other is bankrupt." Other examples he speaks of are a person who is "*both* addicted *and* responsible for it" And that "*both* inner-directed selfishness *and* selflessness constitute mental health."

In our daily lives we try to frame things in this context of both/ and. Just as I finished "interviewing" my husband for the paragraph above, someone called me on the telephone to wish me happy birthday. It was a call of about five minutes. During the call, the person on the phone and I talked mostly about her.

When I got off the phone, my husband commented that it was interesting that this person called to wish me happy birthday and spent the time talking about her self. I quickly added that it was a factor of both me and her. Though this person does often talk about her self, I was aware that I encouraged that as a way of not talking about my self. It wasn't the fault of either her or me; it was *both*.

Another variation on this same theme was taught to me by a favorite graduate school professor. I received a lot of clinical supervision from her while working on my courses for licensure. She suggested that we replace the word "but" with the word "and." For example, "I love my husband, *but* I am mad at him." The construction of this sentence implies that these are separate concepts, and the use of the word "but" almost suggests that being angry with him cancels out loving him or that both can't exist simultaneously. If we instead say, "I love my husband, *and* I am mad at him," we are acknowledging that *both* things are true and present. And both things can exist at the same time. It doesn't have to be one or the other. We need to own both. It is what will help us get well.

Living with *both* is living in the gray and living in the middle. It is not choosing one thing or another or having to be all or nothing. Disentangling is about finding the balance for your self. This is a moment-by-moment process that requires you to be aware of your extremes and to creatively determine what may be a healthier middle ground for you at that time.

As you start on this work, you may find that at first you move from one extreme to the other. For example, you may go from telling someone almost everything to deciding that you won't tell him or her anything anymore. You may skip the middle. My experience is that it is not unusual to do this. We have so little experience living in the gray that we are likely to miss the mark when we first start trying to do this. Once I have jumped from one extreme to the other and become aware of it, then my task is to gradually move my self from this other extreme toward the middle. So, instead of telling this other person in my life absolutely nothing, I gradually learn what I can and cannot safely tell him or her, and then I resume a new and moderated communication pattern with the person. I am living in the gray.

# It's About Intervening on Your Own Behalf

*Intervening on your own behalf* is a phrase I came up with to help clients to understand the essential part they play in their own process of disentangling. In the field of addiction treatment, we do "interventions" on the addict. A group of caring and knowing family and friends get together with the addict, usually with professional help, and confront the addict about his or her disease. Each person then describes specific behaviors about the addict's use that they are worried about and usually tired of. The primary goal of the intervention is to get the addict to go into addiction treatment and thus change his or her addictive behaviors.

*Intervening on your own behalf* is about becoming aware of your own destructive patterns of thought and action and making efforts to change those patterns for the better.

At first, intervening on your self is somewhat hard. The fact that you've bought this book, though, suggests that you have some awareness that you want to make some changes for your self. When clients first come to therapy, they are intervening on their own behalf. Even these first steps of seeking help are self-interventions.

As you progress in separating your self emotionally from the other person, you will hopefully be gaining a clearer picture of who you are and who the other person is. As you learn more about you, you will become more aware of who and what entangles you, what causes you to be entangled, and how you feel and act when you are entangled. With the information and other skills you are developing, you can then start making more informed decisions about whether you want to act/react in the same old ways or you want to do something different.

A goal is to become aware of the moment in which you have this choice, this opportunity. Now, we are given many of these moments over the course of the day. All I am speaking of here is any one of those specific moments when we realize that we are feeling a certain way, talking a certain way, and are about to act/react in our next predictable way. *That* is the moment I am speaking of when we can say to our self, "Oh, I know what's going on here, and I don't want to keep doing this!" *That* is the moment when we can tell our self to stop and to go a different route. Twelve-step programs define insanity as continuing to do the same thing and expecting different results. Let's do something different on our own behalf. Let's intervene on our insanity.

When I am pursuing an argument too far, I am aware that I keep bringing up the same issues, keep asking the other person the same questions, and keep following him or her from room to room. When I start this following-around stuff, I know that's the moment for me to intervene on my own behalf. That's the moment for me to stop my self and walk the other way. That's the moment for me to take a walk, to call a friend, to do whatever helps me to take a break from this argument and to get some healthy distance from it so I can think more clearly and have more serenity. Pursuing this argument will not give me clarity and serenity. I have to remind my self of this.

And I have to be the one to make this change for my self. I am the one who has to have enough awareness and observation of my own thoughts, feelings, and behaviors that I see the opportunity to do something different. And I am the one who has to be developing my own boundaries enough that I can actually *do* something different for my self at that moment.

THE BASICS

# It's About Spiritual Growth

Through my participation in a twelve-step fellowship I have heard that "religion is for people who are afraid of going to hell and spirituality is for people who have been there."

There is no doubt that the process of disentangling involves spiritual growth. Our entanglements have often evolved from our beliefs that we alone can control and create what we want in our relationship with the other. Though we have not necessarily thought of it this way or been aware of these beliefs, our thoughts and actions have reflected our beliefs that if we say or do things in just the right way at just the right time with just the right expression and tone, we can get just what we want from this entangled relationship. We act as though we are in control. As my twelve-step program says, we "force solutions." We believe we have the power to make things happen in the way we'd like them to. We act like we know exactly what is best for us and how things should happen. We act like we're the ultimate power. Either we are in charge or we think the other person with whom we are entangled is a "god" and therefore has the power. And our lives go to hell.

Spirituality is about coming to a belief that there is a power greater than our self and allowing that higher power to be a living presence in our lives.

The process of disentangling is about *both* intervening on your own behalf *and* letting go and letting your higher power act on your behalf.

The important concept here is developing some belief in a power greater than your self. You decide who or what that power is for you. Your higher power may be the God you know through your religious faith. Your higher power may be a personal God you have come to know on your own. You may still be discovering your higher power.

Spiritual growth is about cultivating this belief in a higher power. It can be a wonderful, freeing experience to realize you are not the ultimate one in charge and to learn to let go of things you cannot control to this higher power.

Learning what you can and cannot control is an essential part of this process of disentangling. We start by thinking that we can control most everything, or at least we give it a good try. Then, as we hit our heads against walls, if we are lucky, we begin to see that just maybe we cannot make happen what we want to happen. We can offer to the situation what is reasonable, and then we have to let go and let God.

In talking with people about this, I think of the old saying, "You can lead a horse to water, but you can't make it drink." I use this to help my entangled clients see the limits of what they can do in a situation. We can make an offering, a gift, so to speak, to the other, and then we have to simply stand still and let that person do with it as he or she wishes. We are not the other's higher power. We need to remember that we each have our own higher power.

In order to let go of things beyond our control, it is important to develop faith—faith that we are not alone, faith that a power greater than our self is in fact present and attentive. So when we let go, we are not falling into the abyss of emptiness and darkness; rather, we are relaxing into the arms of a power that is there for us and will provide for us what we really need.

I am reminded of a couple of things we say in my twelve-step program related to this:

> *"What I need to know will come to my attention without any effort on my part."*

> *"What I need will be there for me."*

And I am also reminded of a short prayer I made up one lonely, unhappy Christmas Eve in the second year of my recovery:

> *"God,*
> *If it's me, help me to know.*
> *If it's not, help me to let go."*

As I said this prayer that Christmas Eve outside in the dark of my driveway, I felt comfort and relief. I was not alone. I was not in charge. I was not totally responsible for all the ills of my life and their cures. My higher power was there, too, ready and available to share these self-imposed burdens, to support me and protect me. All that was required of me was to reach out for this spiritual help.

And reaching out for this spiritual help is truly a challenge sometimes. Even as we cultivate our belief in a power greater than our self, it is easy to get caught up in a situation and slip into our super-control behaviors. We may not be aware that once again we are trying to manipulate, manage, or control someone. We may not be aware that again we are acting like we know what is best for all of us.

And so spiritual growth involves not only having the belief that a power greater than your self exists, but also the practice of making contact with that higher power. Daily practice. Moment-to-moment contact, if desired. Through prayer, meditation, monologues, dialogues, writing, walks, contact with nature, time with children, time alone. Whatever helps you to get in touch with your higher power is what I mean by practice.

We get so busy with our daily lives that it is easy to get into our rip-and-run mode and, as an extension of that, to employ our push-and-pull techniques on the people and events in our life. By regularly making our self available to contact with our higher power, we can consciously sort through what we can and cannot control, and we can release our self with comfort and serenity from those things beyond our control.

THE BASICS

# It's a Process without Rules or Sequence

Please notice that the title for the outline on disentangling starts with the word "Ideas." That's what they are: ideas. Yes, carefully thought-through ideas. Ideas that are born of experience and tested through yet more experience. And they are offered only as ideas.

This process of disentangling does not require you to do such-and-such. There is no clear and proper formula for achieving the emotional and personal clarity we are working toward. There is no recipe for success here.

Clients often ask, "What is the *right* thing to say?" "What is the *right* thing to do?" "Do you think I did *the right thing*?"

Well, I don't know.

The more helpful question to ask our self is "Did I listen to me and respond in a way that is true to what I heard from me?" "Did I speak or act in a way that respected both the other's needs as well as my own?"

Those of us who get entangled are often people who do want to do things the right way. We want very much to please others, and we certainly don't want to create any conflict. Avoiding conflict is extremely important, and many of our decisions about what to say and do may be based on this drive to keep things running smoothly.

So it is no surprise that questions come up for us like "Should I . . .?" "Was it okay that I . . .?" "Was it wrong for me to . . .?"

The process of disentangling, however, has no rules. There are no "shoulds" or "should nots." The process of disentangling is about finding the answers for your self. It's about creating emotional space for you so you can listen to your needs and feelings and thoughts. Granted, this may be listening to you for the first time in your life, or you may have limited experience in listening to you. So, at first, you may not be hearing much or you may not be aware of what you are hearing. And this may press you to ask, "Now what should I do?"

Well, the process involves your continuing to listen to you— talk to "knowing" others, do some writing, have some quiet time—so that you can figure out what is the thing *you* need to say or to do. Disentangling is a process that is inviting us to move from being focused on the external to focusing on the internal, to move away from external expectations and directions to internal feelings and thoughts that truly provide much of the information we seek.

A client came to see me just today with these issues. She entered therapy because she has been having a hard time letting go of a romantic relationship. For the past three years she had been seeing a man whom she had met through her colleagues in her law firm. The first two years of the relationship were enjoyable and mutual. Over this past year, however, he has distanced himself from her in major ways. In essence, they are no longer seeing each other and are barely talking. My client does not understand this change and has been reluctant to accept it. Today she is wondering whether to send this man a card congratulating him on the promotion he has just received at his work.

There is no right or wrong answer for this woman in this case. She will have to figure out what it is that's best for her. We talk about her question in this way. We look at her motivations for wanting to send the card. We look at possible expectations she may have if she sends the card. We look at what her message to him would be if she sent the card. In the end, she says she guesses she won't send the card if it upsets *her* too much. She will keep listening to her self to decide this.

And so we are again living in the gray. In the absence of rules and prescriptions, we have to figure out many of these answers for our self. And while we do, we are in the gray. There are not necessarily many yes-or-no answers. It is not often appropriate or helpful to simply say, "Do this/Don't do that." So we have to live a while with wondering and not knowing. And while we do this, we just keep focusing on our self and making contact with our higher power.

In this same way, there is no proper sequence of steps for disentangling. Yes, my outline of ideas is written in a specific order. Most of this order is for clarity and logic. It was even difficult to decide in what order to present them to you. It is necessary to face our illusions before we can work on detachment and boundaries. Our illusions can keep talking us back into our hopes and dreams and further away from realities. Our spiritual growth is equally important to this process. Some people have suggested that spirituality should be listed first on the outline. I understand this reasoning as well.

The point is that disentangling involves working with ideas from any of the four sections at any point in time. It involves working with all of the four sections at the same time. This is not a step-by-step process that you proceed through item by item, gratefully checking off what you have completed. What you think you have completed today may be your assignment again tomorrow. These issues keep coming up, and we keep returning to these ideas for disentangling and apply them situation by situation.

Hopefully, as you go through this process of disentangling, you will feel less lost and be more quickly able to find you, your higher power, and your new skills and awareness. This will come to you as you work simultaneously with your illusions, detachment, boundaries, and spirituality. They all interrelate. They are all equally important. Our growth comes from working in all of these areas in no particular order other than the order that we find best meets our needs in a particular situation at a particular moment.

THE BASICS

# It's a Process That Takes Time

Recently I was in America's "largest gift shop" on an East Coast beach. On a shelf were attractive sand sculptures. One of them was a wizard in a flowing royal-purple robe holding a glowing emerald-green crystal ball. I was charmed by the sculpture and thought of getting it to put in my office, essentially as a friendly, ironic comment on the process of changing our self.

We'd like to think we can change our self in an instant. We want and sometimes even need a quick cure. Just the week before, I had felt a need to explain to a new client the limits of my services. She seemed to have some idea of my being able to do great things to transform her life. I had explained to her that I was not in any form a wizard working magic.

Rather, I explained to her that I see my self as joining with her on a journey to work on the things that bring her to counseling. I explained that I believe that many of the answers she seeks are already within her, and we can work toward her hearing them and responding to them.

My experience is that this journey takes a good while. In fact, I do not think of it as ending. Rather, it becomes simply the path that we take as we live our lives.

Yes, I believe that we can fairly quickly start seeing things differently and learning new skills to help us make some changes in our life. It is the application of these new learnings that can be slow in coming.

We may start seeing our illusions and attend more to the reality of our situations. That reality may suggest that it is not in our best interest to continue in a particular relationship.

Behaviorally, however, we may be a long way from being able to act on this new understanding. We may well continue in the relationship until we have more clarity, greater detachment, better boundaries, and stronger spirituality. That is what we need to do. And that is okay.

We need to be patient with our self. We need to stay on our path of healing as best we can, and we need to kindly reassure our self that we are doing the best we can as fast as we can. As the twelve-step programs remind us, we were not made this way in a day, so we cannot expect to become different in a day.

Actually, many of us have had our entangling thoughts and behaviors for years. They have been the very way we see and respond to the world. If we are a people-pleaser, we have sought to please most everyone we have come in contact with, from parents to teachers to bosses to our dentist. If we tend to avoid conflict and, in so doing, ignore our own needs, we have tended to do this in most settings and with most people. These styles of thinking, feeling, and behaving are ingrained. That is why it has been so hard for many of us to see them in the first place.

So, making changes that create more balance and serenity in our lives is really a major overhaul of our systems. Twelve-step thinking is different from that which most of us have been used to. It does involve a "brainwashing" of sorts, a most refreshing washing, actually. And this brainwashing takes time.

Disentangling is about this same process of deep changes. It is about learning to become aware of our self when for years our focus has been outside our self. It is about seeing our self as a being separate from and relating to others when for years we have been entangled. It is about setting boundaries when for years we have had none. It is about living with and turning over to our higher power things that we have no control over when for years we've been trying to do it all on our own.

These changes cannot be had quickly. There is no wizard. There is no wizard on my office shelf, either. I decided against the ironic joke, though the wizard was truly lovely and inviting, as is the desire for a quick, miraculous cure.

The important reality is that these changes *can* be had. *We* can transform our lives. *We* can make these deep changes. We just need to be patient and realistic with our self as we travel on this journey. We need to see our smaller successes as we go along. They will be there. They may not be the larger successes you think you want. It is important to see them and honor them as they occur. They are the stepping-stones in your journey. If you don't see them and honor them, you may lose your way. If you see and honor them, they will help you with your next step.

Disentangling is a process that takes time. It may take a longer time than you wish, but it is worth every bit of time that it takes. We are transforming our lives. Hopefully, as the changes come, piece by piece, we will reach a point where we can never go back to how we used to be. And making such changes really does take a while.

THE BASICS

# Every Day Ain't Great

Every Day Ain't Great is a cousin of the previous basic, It's a Process That Takes Time. Part of the reason that it can take a good while to make these changes in our lives is the reality that we won't do everything perfectly the first time. We won't have insights and then be able to run right out and successfully apply them.

We will make mistakes. We will know what we want to do for our self in a situation and find that we "blow it." We will successfully set a limit with someone one day, only to find that we can't set a similar limit with someone else the next day. We will have days that feel just like the old days when we are agitated, preoccupied, and anxious. We will think poorly of our self and tell our self we've learned nothing.

This is a warning: Not every day and every interaction will show your progress. This is normal. Be not discouraged. The twelve-step programs tell us: "Two steps forward. One step back."

To expect that *every* day can be great is unrealistic. It is symptomatic of our black-and-white thinking, our gravitation toward all or nothing. Facing this reality can be sad. We'd really like for things to go well all the time.

In the early 1980s my husband and I were visiting his family's home on a lake in Maine. One day while there, we rented an aluminum boat with a small motor, and we gently cruised from Naples at our end of the lake to Harrison at the other end. The day was gorgeous, with blue skies and warm sun. We were in no hurry and dawdled along as we wished, checking out islands and bays and houses and wildlife. We enjoyed each other's company, comfortably sharing chat and silence. It was a great day. I have often wished that every day could be like that, and in a friendly, fun way I have adopted the reminder that "Every day ain't a boat trip to Harrison."

No, every day isn't a sunny, relaxed trip in a boat. In fact, if you will bear with me while I extend this metaphor, there have also been many days when I have said, "I am not going down with this ship!" There are days when I feel insecure, anxious, discouraged. I believe that at any moment I may lose the things that are important to me. Sometimes reality suggests that bad things may indeed happen, that in fact the ship may sink. These are not great days. In fact, they can be downright difficult. The goal is not to drown. Let the ship go down, but don't be on it.

What is important is to start to see the path you are on as you move from entanglements to centeredness and serenity. The path is not a straight line. It has curves and detours and obstacles. The path may have curves that are like switchbacks going up a mountain. You may have traveled a long way and find that you have not gained that much altitude. You may come around a curve and be stopped immediately by something in your path. Your journey is slowed down.

There are boat trips that start out with warm and sunny conditions. The sky is blue, the water calm, the mood relaxed. And then, out of what seems to be nowhere, appears a dark and ominous thunderstorm that comes and creates turbulence and unrest.

Our path is what is constant through all of this. Our path consists of what we are learning about our self, what we are coming to understand about our entanglements, and the things we are learning in order to help our self detach, set boundaries, and develop our spirituality. Our path is our focus on our self and our relationship with our higher power.

Your path will be your personal path. Not one of us has exactly the same one. Our paths reflect our uniqueness. Your path will be cultivated by you. Certainly this book is offering some ideas on the general construction of your path, but it is yours to create.

Sometimes your path will be clearer than others. Sometimes you may be stopped for a while to determine the next direction to take. The good news, though, is that hopefully you will not feel lost again in the way you did when you were entangled.

My experience is that not every day is great. I make mistakes and have setbacks. My experience is also that even when this happens, I am able to find my self again much quicker than in the past. And I do not feel lost. I understand what I have done, and I understand what I can do to retrieve my peace and clarity.

# Don't Go This Alone

Entanglements invite us to isolate. We become so focused on the other person that we drop everything else. We decline opportunities with friends. We decline opportunities with our self. We skip out on our responsibilities to work, to our family, to our previous commitments. At a certain point there seems to be nothing more important than whatever is or is not going on with that other person.

And so we become isolated. And that isolation adds to our craziness. Without input from sources outside the problem, our thinking can get more obsessive and irrational. We can't seem to think of much other than that in which we are entangled. And often our contacts with that person with whom we are entangled add to our craziness rather than untangle it. He or she say things to us and about us that we either totally adopt or totally discount. After a conversation with the person with whom we are entangled, it is easy for us to end up feeling like we are the problem completely. We feel worse and more confused than when we began.

We want to believe that we can talk to the person with whom we are entangled and resolve the things we want to resolve. And so we repeatedly go to them to talk once more about all of this. And once more we find our self tangled and stuck.

It doesn't even dawn on us to go talk to someone else.

Talking with someone else can help us to free our self from this tangled web. Talking with someone else does not mean having him or her tell you what to do. Rather, it means discussing your issues, listening to what is said back, and then doing with the discussion whatever you may.

Talking with someone else helps to break up our thoughts and thus create new and different thoughts and possibilities. Talking with someone else can give us new ideas, can help us see things in a new light, and can help us to see things more objectively, more realistically. No doubt our perceptions have become distorted. We have adjusted and adjusted to unacceptable situations and behaviors. In order to do this, we have to have altered our perceptions. An outside reality check can be most useful in making adjustments in our perceptions.

Talking with someone else can also help us not feel so alone. As our isolation has increased, so has our loneliness. In part this is ironic. We think we are pursuing this entangled relationship because we want to be in a relationship and have companionship. The reality is often, however, that we are lonely in the entangled relationship. It provides little to no good, healthy companionship.

We may also feel lonely because we tell our self all sorts of unhealthy things. We tell our self that:

* No one would understand my problem or situation.

* No one else has this problem.

* This is stupid that I have this problem.

* I am too embarrassed to tell anyone about this situation.

* I can handle this on my own.

* It's too late to do anything about this problem now.

* I'm not supposed to talk to anyone outside my family about my troubles.

* Other people may be nice and listen, but they really don't care.

* I tried this before but it didn't help.

* No one can help me.

Between our entangled relationship and our own trapping thoughts, we have become stuck. Reaching out to others can help to change this.

It is important to be selective as you pick these people with whom to talk. Toby Rice Drews addresses this very well in *Getting Them Sober, Volume 1*. She speaks of the need for us to talk to people who understand the difficulties of entanglements, addictions, and relationships. If we talk to people who don't understand our experiences, we are likely to get unhelpful advice, biased points of view, and plain old gossip. None of this helps us to disentangle. In fact, it can often complicate things more for us. We become even more confused and angry and sad and hopeless.

You will have to find the people who are "in the know." It is likely that these people are not your family members or best friends. Though frequently these people in our lives love us and are honestly and deeply concerned about us and want good things for us, they often do not know what to say that will help us to disentangle. Their suggestions of "hang in there" or "give it another try" are words of encouragement that may not be in your best interest if you really stop and tune in to that. Messages like "You don't want to upset so-and-so by doing something like that" suggest that we need to consider the needs of someone else more than our own. Disentangling involves considering our own needs as equal if not more important as we work out these difficulties.

So where are these people "in the know"? They are certainly in twelve-step groups—both for those struggling with addiction and for those whose family members and significant others are struggling. There are free support groups available in most communities in the United States and in countries around the world. The Al-Anon/Nar-Anon welcome statement indicates that living with addiction can be too much for us as individuals. Living with an entanglement can similarly be too much for most of us. We cannot handle it alone. The experience, strength, and hope of the members of these fellowships can help us to recover. We are not told what to do in these groups. Rather, we gather information and inspiration and then use them in our lives as we wish and as we can.

Other people "in the know" are in the helping professions. They may be psychotherapists, addiction counselors, medical professionals, or ministers. It is important to not assume, though, that any of these people would understand your experiences simply because of their professional title. It is important for you to be a shopper for the services you seek. It is okay for you to inquire about a professional's credentials and areas of interest and expertise. Just because someone is a psychologist does not mean that he or she works well with addiction. The individual may not understand the experience of entanglement and the difficulties of extraction. Interview each one you are considering. Let him or her know what you are looking for. Decide if he or she is the one to help you find and keep you.

Support groups can be another place to find healthy companionship. These groups may be offered by public and private mental health and addiction treatment programs and clinicians. Sometimes these groups are also held in churches or are started by a grassroots group of individuals who share these issues. These groups may have in their names words like relationship addictions, healthy relationships, codependency, or loving too much. Whatever the title, I suggest you visit the group or participate in an intake session with a group leader and gather information that will help you to decide if this group of people could be helpful to you.

Lastly, individuals can be of great support to us if they are patient and understanding of the complexity of our entanglements. These individuals may be select friends or family members, individuals from twelve-step programs whom we have asked to be our sponsor, or anyone else who happens into our life that we feel truly understands us and our situation.

Regardless of the messages you give to your self, you are not unusual or alone in what is happening to you. There are people out here who can join you in your efforts to disentangle. There is no need to do it alone. In fact, it is very hard to disentangle successfully on your own.

Joining with others on this journey can be freeing and fun.

I invite you to join us.

"Each of these elements is very important to me, and I find them to be interwoven."

# 7 The Four Areas of Work

*"Each of these elements is very important to me, and I find them to be interwoven. This is not a step one/step two process. I use each of them, with awareness or not, situation by situation. When I look back at something that happened, I can see, for example, how I detached, set some boundaries, and reminded my self of the reality of the situation."*

*Rebecca, age 18*

This chapter offers a detailed look at each of the specific *Ideas on How to Disentangle* that were presented in Chapter Five, "The Big Picture." This chapter is divided into the four sections described on the *Ideas* list: Facing Illusions, Detaching, Setting Healthy Boundaries, and Developing Spirituality. Within each of these sections, each idea on the *Ideas* list on that topic is presented and then followed with comments that describe what I have in mind about that idea.

The comments about each idea come from several sources. The comments are in part things that I say as I explain the ideas to my self and to my clients. The comments are based on experiential activities we do in group and individual therapy sessions and the results that come from those activities. The comments are also based on the experiences of my clients as they work on releasing their selves from their entanglements.

All the comments have been deeply influenced by the practicing of the words on the page by my self and many others.

I have attempted to offer the information in a brief, easily referenced form. Feel free to jump around as you read the ideas. Read the ideas that seem to apply to you most at the time. Read the ideas that attract your interest. Read the ideas that may confuse you or that you don't get. Read them in whatever order you desire. Do read them all.

Remember, these are the nuts and bolts of helping our self to disentangle from someone else. They are the ingredients that can transform our lives from anxiety and obsession to serenity and centeredness.

Try these ideas on. See what works for you. As you do, remember the general concepts about the process of disentangling presented in Chapter Five, "The Basics." Remember, this is a process that focuses on you. This is a process about finding balance in your life. This is a process that involves you listening to you and your situation and figuring out what works best for you. This is a process that involves belief in a power greater than your self.

Blending these ideas on how to disentangle with an understanding of how the process works, you can create a stronger and healthier you.

"You know, I think she's changed.
I don't think that will happen again."

*Trish, age 21*

# Facing Illusions

*"Oh, what a tangled web we weave,*
*When first we practise to deceive!"*

Sir Walter Scott (*Marmion:* Canto VI, Stanza 17)

How true these famous lines ring in terms of the entanglements I speak of.

In the case of our tangled webs, the deceiving we do is to our self. We create all sorts of illusions or false beliefs about the other person and about our self. Our illusions may also be called fantasies, dreams, and hopes.

Illusions are usually about what we think things are or what we want them to be rather than the reality of what they are. And not only do we repeatedly create these illusions in our relationships, but we also become attached to them and are hard-pressed to let them go.

So, in order to disentangle our self, we must get in touch with the reality of our situation. In order to free our self from the "stuckness" of our entanglements, we must find the truth and work with our self to accept it. Doing this can help us begin to get some emotional distance from other people and our situations with them and can help us to start seeing things in a new way.

FACING ILLUSIONS
# Find the Truth About Your Situation

*". . . and the truth shall make you free."*

John 8:32

The truth may set us free, *and* it may be hard to find.

Without our awareness, we live in our thoughts, our ideas, our hopes, our dreams. "Things will be so much better when . . ." says a client to me.

We believe that though things may not be great today, they will be better tomorrow. "Though I'm starving today, one day I will sit at a great feast," explained another client.

We live with the hopes that others will change in the way we'd like them to. "I just know he'll treat me differently this time," says yet another client.

The disease of addiction is characterized by denial—denial that the specific manifestation of addiction is causing the individual and his or her family problems.

Entanglements, too, are characterized by denial—denial that our unrealistic expectations, our inaccurate perceptions, and our fantasies about the other person are causing us problems.

We need to see others for who they are here and now.

We need to pay attention to words *and* behaviors.

If we are unclear about things, we can ask for clarity.

We can stop making excuses, defending, and rationalizing.

We can live in the present and pay attention to all that is being said and done. Much of the truth we seek is right here now.

The truth is not necessarily bad. In fact, the truth may even be good news. It's just that often the truth is *different* from what we thought or understood. As a client of mine frequently says, "I want to get into the reality."

Without the truth, we remain entangled. Our illusions can feed our hopes and dreams of controlling and changing things beyond our control. Our illusions take us into our fantasies and away from the reality of our lives.

Finding the truth is a necessary step in finding our self.

### FACING ILLUSIONS
# Work to Accept the Truth You Find

*"The truth will set you free . . .*
*but first it will piss you off!"*

Bumper sticker on my friend's suitcase

Yes, once we've found the truth, it may make us mad. It may make us sad. We may have trouble believing it.

I have found that working to accept the truth can be like working through the process of grieving. That process involves fundamental components: denial, anger, bargaining, depression, and acceptance. This process and its components apply not only to death, but to many different kinds of losses and changes in our lives.

Finding and accepting the truth about our situation is also a loss. Regardless of whether the truth is good news or bad news, it is *a change*. It involves letting go of beliefs and hopes and dreams. It involves saying good-bye to what we thought things were or could be.

No wonder we may resist facing our illusions. Not only are they essential to our entanglements, but they are also emotionally difficult to release.

Facing our illusions often does not feel good at first. So we may resist this change in a variety of ways, including readopting illusions, blaming others, blaming our self.

It is often only over the long haul that accepting the truth feels good and freeing. But that is the way to free our self from our entanglements: working to find and accept the truth about our situation as we are willing and able, over and over again.

FACING ILLUSIONS

# Illusions and You

**Think of a person or situation in
which you presently feel entangled.**

**What is a present illusion of yours
relative to this person or situation?
What is a hope or belief you are holding
about this person or situation that may
or may not be really happening?**

**What has happened that makes you
believe your illusion may be true?**

**What has or has not happened that tells
you your illusion may not be true?**

**Looking at this data, what is the reality
about this person and/or your situation?**

**How are you feeling about this
reality you are finding?**

"Everything that's happened
wrong is my fault."

*Anne, age 29*

# Detaching

*"'What do you want on your pizza?' I was asked. I don't
know. I couldn't think. I just used to go along with what he
wanted rather than try to decide what goes on a pizza that
I would like."*

*Charlotte, age 34*

Detachment is a word I have come to know through my
twelve-step program, which defines it as a recovery tool.
Detachment means that I am not responsible for the addiction
or recovery of the other person. I can let go of my attachments
to trying to manage/fix/control his or her addiction and live
my own life.

Detachment in this sense means not suffering because of others,
not allowing my self to be used or abused by others, and not
doing for others what they can do for their self. Detaching
allows me to see things more realistically and make decisions
that are ultimately better for me and the other person.

Indeed, I think of detachment as a way to back off of a situation
so that I can bring it into focus and see it more clearly. Until
I detach, I am right up in the face of the situation, or perhaps
literally up in the face of the individual with whom I'm
entangled. This type of contact leaves me with blurred vision
and a narrow and often distorted perception.

Detachment enables me to better see reality.

Detachment is not necessarily about leaving the other person physically, though sometimes this is the best thing to do either at the moment or permanently. This section on detachment, however, is directed at helping you to get emotional separation for your self. Then you can see much better what's going on and decide about the issue of physical separation.

The ideas listed in this section are specific things we can do in our interactions with others to help us get this distance. They are some "how-tos" of detaching. It is only partially useful to say to people that they should not allow their self to be used or abused if they do not know how to make this happen. These ideas on detachment aim to help us to know what to do in order to not suffer, to not be used/abused, and to not do for others what they can do for their self.

The ideas involve looking at our self and our vulnerability to entanglements. Understanding these things about our self and our history can help us to become less vulnerable.

The ideas also involve changes in the ways we interact with others. When detaching, we slow down our interactions and work toward acting rather than reacting to others.

All of the ideas involve learning more about our self, learning to listen to our self as we interact with others, and protecting both our serenity and our feeling that we have both feet firmly on the floor and cannot be knocked off-balance.

DETACHING

# Become Aware of Who and What Entangles You

* With whom do you get entangled?

* What entangles you with him or her?

* What parts of you get entangled?

* How do you act and feel when you're entangled?

Detaching is about getting emotional distance from a person or situation.

In order to detach, we need to first become aware of with whom and what we may be entangled. The above four questions are all interrelated. They are all about this awareness-raising within us.

The more we understand what in us makes us vulnerable to entanglements, the more we can take care of our self. The more aware and knowing we become, the more we can intervene on our own behalf.

We can better understand our vulnerabilities to entanglements by looking at what happened to us as we grew up. It is useful to look at how people treated us and how we reacted to their treatment. What did we learn about our self then? What did we learn about others? How did we cope? Survive? Develop?

I find it useful to use a couple of tools in helping clients to look at some of their earlier experiences that likely relate to their entanglements today.

Janet Woititz's 1983 book *Adult Children of Alcoholics, Expanded Edition* broke new ground in defining a list of characteristics shared by adult children of alcoholics (see Appendix A).

Although *Adult Children of Alcoholics* was written with a specific focus on the children of alcoholics, subsequently it has become clear that this material also applies to the full range of family dysfunction. Anyone who grew up with addiction in any form—alcohol or other drugs, gambling, or overeating; chronic mental and/or physical illness; extreme and rigid religious attitudes; or was adopted, lived in foster care, or in other potentially dysfunctional family systems—can identify with the characteristics Woititz described.

Studying this list invites us to look at our own characteristics. Are we people-pleasers? Are we super-responsible or super-irresponsible? Do we need full control? Are we too serious? How do these features of ours relate to our entanglements?

Perhaps we are entangled because the people-pleasing part of us believes we haven't yet done *the* right thing that will please the other.

Perhaps we are entangled because the super-responsible part of us believes we have not done enough, have not tried hard enough to make things work.

Perhaps we are entangled because we feel guilty when we do try to back off emotionally.

Understanding our roles in our family of origin can also be useful. Sharon Wegscheider-Cruse describes these roles in her book *Another Chance: Hope and Health for the Alcoholic Family* (see Appendix B). She presents four sibling roles taken on in a family: Hero, Scapegoat, Lost Child, and Mascot.

Studying these roles can help us see the role or roles characteristic of our self, and we can see to what extent we may be playing out these roles in our entangled relationships.

Perhaps we were the caretaker and are trying to care-take in our entangled relationship.

Perhaps we were the funny, entertaining character and are trying to laugh and joke away our unhappiness with a relationship.

As Wegscheider-Cruse explains, these roles in and of themselves are not bad. It's our rigid attachment to them that locks us in and keeps us from acting from our internal self.

What we are seeking is to be able to listen to our self and to the situation at hand and then to choose our response from what we hear rather than from old, external scripts written by us and for us a long time ago.

DETACHING

# Entanglements and You

**Look at Janet Woititz's characteristics
of adult children of alcoholics in
Appendix A. Mark those characteristics
with which you identify.**

**Look at Sharon Wegscheider-Cruse's
family roles described in Appendix B.
Mark the roles with which you identify.**

**Now, think of someone with whom you are entangled:**

What entangles you with this person?

What parts of you make you vulnerable to
an entanglement with this person?

Are you playing out any old,
rigid roles with this person?

How do you feel when you are entangled?

How do you act when you are entangled?

DETACHING
# Separate Your Problem(s) from the Other Person's Problem(s)

When we are entangled, it can be hard to determine where we stop and where the other person begins. We are sort of mushed up together and stuck there. In both physical and emotional ways, there is little to no space between us.

So, it should be no surprise that we take responsibility for things that we are not responsible for, that we truly believe we know what's best for the other person, and that we allow our emotions to be so affected by his or her moods and behaviors.

We are a tangled mess.

Mentally separating the pieces of you from the enmeshed "us" is important to detaching. This involves literally creating two separate lists: your problem(s) and the other's problem(s). Now, as the twelve-step programs say, we're not trying to "take his or her inventory." We are not trying to solve his or her problems. We are, however, trying to surgically remove pieces of our self from this heap so we can do something about our problem.

Too often we are taking way too much responsibility for our relationship working or not.

Too often we personalize things the other person says or does, believing we are at fault, believing we are the one with the problem.

Learning to separate our issues and problems from the other person is essential to detaching. It allows us to see much more clearly what we can and cannot control in our relationship. It allows us to start seeing a self both in a relationship and separate from it.

DETACHING

# Don't Try to Fix the Other Person's Problem(s)

A logical extension of separating our self and our problems from the other person's is letting go of trying to fix his or her problem(s).

Sometimes it is obvious that we are trying to fix someone else's problems. We try to stop our loved one from drinking or drugging. We look for jobs for him. We take her to doctors, to counselors, to church.

Less obvious, but equal in our intentions to fix people, are behaviors such as lending them money, buying them clothes and possessions, and accepting their excuses for their irresponsibility.

Even less obvious attempts to fix others include efforts to cheer them up, efforts to motivate and encourage them, and efforts to keep them from being mad at us.

Sometimes we even try to fix problems of others that really aren't problems: "I bet you're cold. Let me turn up the heat." "I know you must be hungry. . . . Here. Eat."

In our oceanfront efficiency I just said to my eight-year-old daughter, "I bet you can't see out the window well enough (it was a full-length, double sliding door). Let me get you a pillow." She had been just fine with her view. She had not had a problem with it. *I* wanted her to have a "better" view. And how did I know what her view was, anyway?

A good friend of my husband's really helped me to get this "not-fixing-others'-problems" even more clearly. We were visiting his friend in his North Carolina home. A bunch of us were getting into cars to go hear music downtown. I was already in the car with our friend waiting for my husband to join us. I said, "He seems to be in a bad mood, and I don't know what's going on."

Our friend matter-of-factly replied, "Well, if he has a problem he'll have to let us know."

What brilliance!

I heard him and heard him well. He didn't know the power of what he said. But that wasn't important. I knew.

This was a *great* idea: Let the other person speak up for his or her self!

We need to let others solve their own problems. We cannot solve them for them. They will have to do this for their self.

We have to let go of our belief that we can fix others.

We have to let go of our belief that fixing others will fix us.

We believe that if we can fix their problems it will fix our problems. That is how entangled we are with them. Yes, some of their problems are in fact causing us some of our problems, but the resolution of their problems alone is not going to produce in us the health and serenity we desire. While it can be difficult to find contentment within ourselves, it is impossible to find it through others.

Let's fix our self.

DETACHING

# Entanglements and You

**Think again of someone with
whom you are entangled.**

**Draw two columns on a piece of paper
separated by a vertical line. At the top
of one column write My Issues/Problems.
At the top of the other column write
His or Her Issues/Problems.**

**Fill in your column as best you can.
If you stumble into items for "His or Her"
column as you do your own, then jot
them down under their column.**

**What are ways you try to fix the other
person's problem(s)? Can you stop
doing any or all of those things?**

**What are things you can do to work
on your own issues and problems?**

DETACHING
# Work for Emotional Distance

When we are entangled we often have almost no emotional distance from other people. What they say and do dramatically affects how we feel and what we do. Their sadness makes us sad. Their anger brings on our anger and/or our regrets, apologies, and guilt. Their discouragement leaves us discouraged.

We react to whatever comes our way in our interactions with other people. They no sooner finish what they are saying than we jump in with our reactions and solutions. We sometimes don't even let them finish what they are saying before we come running forward with our response. And often those responses are intense and angry or forceful: "You jerk! I can't believe you think that!" "I'm sick of you and your crap!" "That does it! I'm leaving (not really)!"

We are so emotionally close to the person with whom we are entangled that our emotional reactions spin out of the web in which we are both entangled. If we are having trouble seeing our self as a separate person with separate issues, then no wonder we are emotionally tangled as well.

Disentangling involves creating emotional space between our self and the other person so we can see him or her more clearly, hear him or her more clearly, and listen to our self before we act, not react.

We want to move from our style of impulsive reacting to centered acting. We want to create the time and space to absorb what we are hearing from the other person and our self and then, with both feet on the ground and our heart and head clear, offer to the other person our true and honest response.

It is not useful for us to simply give back to the other person what we think he or she wants to hear. It is not useful for us to blast him with our anger and threats. It is not useful for us to repeatedly apologize and throw our self at her mercy.

It is useful for us to emotionally back off and process things before we respond. It is useful to make sure we are listening both to the other person *and* to our self when we are deciding how to act.

As I have gotten older, my eyesight has gotten worse. In order to read words on a page without my glasses, I need to move the paper much farther away from my eyes. As I do this, the letters become clearer to me and then the words appear and then the meanings of the sentences follow.

So it is with getting emotional distance. As we back up, we can see the person with whom we are entangled much more clearly. We can hear what he or she is saying and see the bigger picture. In so doing, we are more calm and centered and able to see and understand our situation with more clarity and meaning.

The following three sections offer specific ideas on how to achieve this emotional distance.

# Observe the Other

**Observe the other more than fully interact
with them—loss of your self is likely if you
get fully into the other's interaction.**

What I have in mind when I suggest observing here is a modified version of watching television, a movie, or a play. When we engage in these activities, we sit back with some physical and emotional distance and take in the data that is coming to us. We listen carefully and often reflectively. We do not sit there waiting to offer an immediate response to what we are hearing. Granted, we may be having reactions, even strong reactions, but we are keeping them to our self as we take in and process the stream of data. We are quiet, attentive, and thoughtful. We may even be aware of things we are feeling and thinking as the external information is presented to us.

But we do not jump up out of our seats and react. Rather, we remain relatively centered and able to continue to receive and process what we are hearing.

My twelve-step program suggests that we say things like we are the evening news, simply announcing things in a matter-of-fact, reporting style. I am suggesting that we also listen as though we are watching the evening news, listening with interest, objectivity, patience, and nonjudgment.

And we need to listen with an observing style that reminds us not to take what the person is saying personally. The evening news is not personal. Neither is a lot of what someone else may be saying to us. Oh, we take it personally. We take most everything personally. But really, what the other person is saying to us may in fact be more about his or her self than about us. As we back off from the other, creating more physical and emotional space, we will be better able to see what is about us and what is not about us. We will see that we don't need to take it all personally.

It's when we take it personally that we lose our self in the interaction with the other person. At that point, we jump up out of our seats and react, unlike our behavior in a theater. We react and speak impulsively. We say things we don't mean and later regret. We talk in circles and repeat our forced points.

My experience of this event is that the floor drops out from underneath me, and I have no ground under my feet. I am free-falling and grabbing onto anything and everything I can to convince, defend, defame, and control.

I can keep my feet on the ground and my self more centered if I work toward this observing style in a conscious way. In my interactions with certain others, I have come to be aware of specific behaviors and/or ways of speaking on the part of the other person that are warning signs to me that I may be about to hear something from him or her that may upset me in some way. When I notice this sign, I consciously enter the conversation with reminders to my self to "Just listen. . . . Stay calm. . . . Observe. . . . Think before responding. . . . Don't feel pressure to answer questions or requests immediately. . . . Breathe. . . . Stay with my self."

As I have said, these reminders are conscious and help me to balance out the interaction so as not to completely get lost in the other person and what he or she is saying. I can actually feel my self creating emotional distance as I remind my self of these things. I am creating a safety zone for my self that allows me to participate in the interaction in ways that allow me to keep my feet on the floor, my head on my shoulders, my emotions under *my* control, and my spirit well and strong.

# Act, Don't React

**Try to act out of your centeredness and not out of your reactions to the other person.**

I have been using the word "centered" throughout this book. Perhaps this is a good moment to elaborate specifically on its meaning.

I am certainly not unique in suggesting that we find and operate out of our center. This concept is frequently offered in the counseling and self-help worlds. To say more specifically what it means and what the experience of centeredness may be like seems useful here.

*Merriam-Webster's Collegiate Dictionary* initially offers this basic definition of "centered": "to place or fix at or around a center or central area or position . . . to give a central focus or basis." It then defines "centered" in a way more specific to my use of the word here: "emotionally stable and secure."*

By disentangling, we are cultivating a self that we may see as our "center." Our self is the core of us. It is the heart of who we are. It is the place where we go to listen to our thoughts, our feelings, and our needs. It is the place that is aware of our physical, mental, emotional, and spiritual lives.

When we have grown up people-pleasing, people-watching, and, in general, externally focused, we tend to be unaware of our self, of our center. We may not even have much of a self. It is common in my therapy work with clients to find that, when they have the opportunity to let go of thinking about what the other person wants, needs, or thinks, and think about their own wants, needs, and thoughts, they draw a big blank. I have seen clients look me straight in the eye with a very lost look and say, "I have *no* idea what *I* want."

In a more extreme form, I have heard clients say that without a focus on others and without straightforward feedback from others about them, they feel like they are not really there. They feel like they don't exist.

---

* By permission. From Merriam-Webster's Collegiate® Dictionary, Eleventh Edition ©2010 by Merriam-Webster, Incorporated (www.Merriam-Webster.com).

And that is what can happen when we lose our self in others. We feel as if we have no center from which to operate on our own behalf. We don't even think of factoring in our self as we interact with the other person. As someone said in a meeting recently, "Where was *I* in the formula?"

Centeredness means that we maintain/return our focus to us, to our self. We can catch our self with our focus out there on others, watching for their reactions, their moods, their behaviors. We can catch our self trying to figure out what they are thinking or what they may need.

We need to turn those very questions back onto our self. We need to ask our self what *we* are thinking and needing. We need to watch our own moods and behaviors. This builds centeredness. Piece by piece, we cultivate that self by returning our focus to us and staying close to our self.

Centeredness is not only returning the focus to our self. It is also a particular feeling. When I am centered, I simply feel better. When I am *reacting* to someone or something, I feel off-balance. I want to act in extremes. I either want to jump in and solve this problem now, and I mean right now, or I want to withdraw into sulking silence. When I am reacting, I am often impulsive in words or deeds that I later regret and for which I may spend much time cleaning up. I add guilt to my desperation.

When I am acting out of my centeredness, I feel much more balanced and secure with my self. Though I am not necessarily relaxed, I do feel less stressed than when I am impulsively reacting. There is an inner calmness and clarity that is my anchor.

In situations where we are letting our focus be on the other, it is important to repeatedly pause and check in with our self. Ideally, we would not have totally left our self out in the first place. But many of us are starting out at square one or two with our development of our self. So we have to listen consciously to the other *and* listen to our self. If you have to take a break and get back with the other person later in order to tune into your self, that's okay. In fact, that has been a useful thing for me to do in order for my self to get clarity and find my own voice.

Centeredness is having a self that we know, that we hear, that we foster, and that we stay close to. When I act out of my centeredness, I am including me in the formula. I am factoring in my thoughts, needs, and feelings as I figure out the answer/ response I truly want to offer to the situation at hand.

# Use Self-Talk

**Use self-talk to help you when you are feeling pulled off of your center (e.g., "I'm okay." "It's okay to say this." "I haven't done anything wrong." "This is not my issue.").**

Self-talk means exactly what it says: talking to your self. Now I imagine you have heard of this behavior as a sign of serious mental illness. Well, in this case I believe it can foster our mental health, assuming we are aware and rational as we talk to our self.

Self-talk is a technique used in cognitive-behavioral psychotherapy. It is a technique used in self-help circles in the form of affirmations. It is a technique used here to help disentangle. In all of these examples, self-talk is used to help us change the way we are thinking so that we are more centered and anchored in reality and honesty.

When we are entangled, our thinking gets all messed up. We get confused, frustrated, and lost. Our focus slips more and more onto other people. We want to know what they think, what they are doing, and what they want.

And so when we talk to others, we want to know what they have to say, and we try to say the things we think they want to hear. Or we say things that we think may produce the results we desire. In any case, we say things that are reactions to the situation and/or are trying to manipulate the situation, rather than things that are true and clear, and that accurately represent our self.

Self-talk is about cultivating an internal dialogue with your self that may be as active as the external dialogue you are having with the other person. While you are standing there talking to someone else, it is important to be checking in with your self as well and perhaps having an actual conversation with your self. For example:

You have asked your spouse if your family, including your spouse, could spend Thanksgiving with your sister's family. You know that your spouse disagrees with your sister on some topics, but she has invited you all to come, and you want to go. So you say:

> David: "Jeanette has asked us to come for Thanksgiving Day. She'll fix the meal if we bring drinks and dessert. What do you think?"

> Susan: "I think that I don't want to go. You should know that. We've been over this too many times already. I actually can't believe you would even consider going. What's wrong with you?"

At this point you may already be feeling pulled off of your center. What you thought was a relatively straightforward question has quickly become fuel for an argument. And you are already feeling on the spot to account for your behavior. Well, STOP for a moment and have a conversation with your self. It could go something like this:

> Self: "My spouse is asking what's wrong with me. Do I think there is anything wrong with me right now?"

> Self: "No, I don't believe there is anything wrong with me right now except that I am feeling uncomfortable with this conversation and the way it is going."

> Self: "Was I wrong to bring up this question?"

> Self: "No, I was not wrong to ask about going to my sister's house. That is an okay thing to do. I want to go, and I'd like it if my spouse would come also."

> Self: "But I know that my spouse is not nuts about my sister."

> Self: "Yes, that is true, but I thought we could at least spend a few hours at her place without any big problems."

> Self: "So what should I say now?"

> Self: "Well, what is true for you now? What is it that *you* want to say to your spouse at this moment?"

> Self: "What is true is that I would like us to go as a family to Jeanette's for Thanksgiving Day."

> Self: "Do you feel like you can say that to your spouse?"

> Self: "I guess so, but it sure makes me nervous."

Having a conversation with our self can really help to get us in touch with our center. We have to ask our self questions about how we feel, what we need, and what we want. Self-talk can help us to clarify things for our self and to fortify our position. This fortification is not in the sense of fighting but rather in the sense of simply accurately representing *us* in a situation.

Self-talk can also be used outside of immediate interactions with others. We can use self-talk to remind our self that it was okay to say or do what we did. We can use self-talk to remind our self that we could not have done anything different in a past situation. We can use self-talk to bring our self into the present moment and out of our thoughts and worries. Self-talk can be used to help us to prepare for future interactions that seem troubling and overpowering for us.

Self-talk is a way to find our center and a technique to help us stay there. In so doing, we are creating emotional distance that helps us to have healthier interactions with others and more stability and clarity for our self.

DETACHING

# Emotional Distance and You

**Think of someone with whom you have recently felt entangled. Perhaps you had an argument with him or her or perhaps you were trying to get him or her to do something or to see something a particular way. Think of a specific interaction you have had with him or her recently that demonstrates this entanglement.**

**With this incident in mind, try to practice these ideas for emotional distance:**

## OBSERVE

Thinking back about your interaction with the other, try to see the other person as though you were watching him on a stage or on the television. Try to imagine your self sitting back and watching and listening to him. What do you hear him saying? How does he sound? What do you observe about his behavior? What are you observing about your self as you listen? What do you notice about your feelings? About your body? About your impulses to act or not to act? About your thoughts? Just observe.

## GET CENTERED

Resisting your impulse to react to the other in what is likely your usual way to respond to her, pause and really tune in to all that you are observing. Make sure you are listening to you, as well as to her. What are you feeling, needing, and wanting in this situation? Find your balance by making sure you are focusing on both the external and the internal. What are you aware of feeling and thinking relative to this specific situation? Can you think of what you really want to do to act, not react, in this situation? Or do you want to act at all at this time? Listen to you.

## SELF-TALK

Go ahead and actually give your self a voice. What do you need to say to you about this situation? What are reminders that you need to say to your self so that you don't get lost in this interaction? What are the points that you want to hold onto, not to force them on the other person but to simply anchor your self in? What are reassurances you can offer your self about you and your needs now? Talk to your self and please listen to what you are hearing.

DETACHING
# Be Aware of Your Motivations

**Be aware of the motivations behind what you say and do in interacting with the other. Make sure you are not saying or doing things to manipulate, control, or change the other or to make him or her feel a certain way or do something specific. You are most likely to keep your centeredness if your motivation is to express your self assertively.**

Being aware of what is motivating me to say and to do things is extremely important. It took me a long time to realize this.

When I started on my journey, I had no awareness of how often I was trying to control or manage others. I had no awareness of my efforts to get the other person to do a wide variety of things that included liking me, doing things I wanted to do, and validating me.

And then, through my own work, I started to see how tangled I would get when I entered a conversation with my own agenda that was basically about trying to manage or control someone else's feelings, reactions, and/or behaviors. I could see how I would repeat my self, say hurtful things, and even "throw in the kitchen sink" in my efforts to get the other person to do something or to even say that he or she understood me.

Most of us don't like to think that we are trying to manage or control others. Robin Norwood boldly laid this out in her book as a characteristic of women who love too much. It was an eye-opener for me. And I have found it to be an eye-opener for my clients as well. Often when I first introduce the notion to them of their trying to control someone else, they reject the idea. We like to think of our self as this sweet person just trying to help.

Well, looking a little deeper, we find that we are not just "trying to help." We are deeply attached to making X, Y, and Z happen for and with the other person, and we are dead serious about it.

Becoming aware of our deeper motivations as we deal with others is an important and necessary first step in helping us to detach.

The Serenity Prayer is a good tool to help us remember our own tendencies toward controlling and the limitations on what we really can and cannot control:

> *God, grant me the serenity to*
> *accept the things I cannot change,*
> *courage to change the things I can,*
> *and the wisdom to know the difference.*

If my motivation is to try to change something I have no control over, I'm headed straight for an entanglement.

Once we are aware of our intentions, then we can decide how we want to express our self. The basic recommendation here is to speak using "I" statements. Be as clear and direct as possible. And have limited attachment to the outcome of what you are saying.

Speak for *you*. Speak for what you believe and need to say relative to the situation at hand. Certainly you may care about what outcome your speaking may bring, but don't get overly attached to it.

If it is a situation that demands a specific thing be done, well, that is a different situation and needs to be handled with clear and meaningful expectations and limits.

The following section on *Setting Healthy Boundaries* will provide many details about ways to express your self assertively and to set necessary boundaries.

For now, it is important to just generally understand that we are going to have greater detachment and fewer entanglements if we are motivated to speak for our self rather than with intentions of trying to change someone else by what we are saying.

After all, it is important to remember that we are in fact separate people with different views and styles. Knowing, seeing, and respecting our separateness and differences is paramount if we are to have healthy relationships.

And with this separateness in mind, it is important to speak up for our self. It is important to say how we feel and what we think. Doing so helps us to feel clearer, calmer, and stronger. And we are communicating a whole lot better, too.

DETACHING

# Motivations and You

**Think of a recent conversation you had with someone that you feel did not go very well. Perhaps you got angry or upset. Perhaps the other person did. Perhaps you simply felt bad about it after it was over.**

What were you trying to communicate
in the conversation?

What were your motivations behind what
you were saying to the other person?

Were you aware of your motivations then?

Were you trying to change the other
person in any way or trying to get him
or her to say or do something?

Was this a situation where the other
person absolutely has to do or say
something, or was that just your desire?

*(continued on page 112)*

Did you get overly attached to the
outcome of the conversation?

Did you find your self saying a variety
of things in a variety of ways to produce
your desired outcome?

Would the conversation have
gone any better if you had:

Used "I" statements?

Been motivated more by simply
representing your own feelings
and needs rather than pulling and
tugging at the other person?

Been less attached to the
outcome of the conversation?

Understood and accepted that we
are all separate human beings with
different thoughts, styles, and outlooks,
and we need to respect those differences
rather than trying to shape things in
our own images and time frames?

> "I just don't understand how we get locked into these arguments. . ."
>
> *Nancy, age 40*

# Setting Healthy Boundaries

*"I just don't understand how we get locked into these arguments and can't just unravel them with love and caring for each other. I get caught up in them . . . and I pursue on and on like I really believe that's going to eventually lead to where I want it to."*

*Nancy, age 40*

Facing our illusions and learning how to detach can help us greatly with disentangling. Allowing our self to back up enough to see the reality of our self, others, and our situations can help us to stop being so consumed with the other person or situation. Just as those of us with aging eyes need reading material to be placed at a distance so we can see the letters and words more clearly, so it is with gaining emotional distance. This, too, helps us to see things more clearly and, hopefully, accurately.

But often facing illusions and detachment are not enough to leave us feeling that we have a strong, clear, and healthy self. They are essential starting points for disentangling and cultivating a healthy self, but frequently we often also need to set boundaries.

This need for boundaries became clear to me as I worked with a client several years ago. She had initially come to see me because her relationship with her husband left her feeling confused and inadequate. In their interactions, she usually felt like she was wrong or had done something wrong. Through her work she learned to not fall prey to this response but rather to detach, observe, listen, and process things for her self. She started to see more clearly what her part in their problems was and was not. She started to feel better.

But one day she called me on an emergency basis. She had had a major argument with her husband and was feeling lost again. The argument had been over her accountability to him. He was angry because he had called her from his out-of-town job, and she was not at home when he called. They had no agreement about a calling time. He accused her of cheating on him and demanded that she stay at home all of the time and be available for his calls. Further, he insisted that when he was back at home she make no plans other than to be available to him.

We talked about this situation. She was able to fairly quickly find her detachment skills and get a better look at what had happened. But she still felt bad, angry, and hopeless. It was clear that for her to continue to grow and for the health of this relationship, she really needed to start setting some reasonable boundaries for her self and her husband. Now that she could see things more realistically, she could start doing this. She needed to learn that it is okay to set boundaries. She needed to figure out which of his demands she would meet and which she would not. She needed to learn how to assert those boundaries and stick by them. She was clearly into the next phase of her growth.

So what does this "setting boundaries" mean? Setting boundaries does not mean establishing walls that cut us off from others. It does not mean rigidly attaching our self to rules and procedures that don't necessarily apply or work in all situations.

Setting boundaries does mean establishing some limits for your self of what you will and won't tolerate in a particular situation. Setting boundaries means that you are able to listen to your self, know your limits, and firmly assert those limits to your self and the other person.

Setting boundaries is really a healthy, friendly thing to do. It helps us to know the parameters of our relationships and interactions. Without letting someone know what your boundaries are, how is that person to know what is and is not okay with you? It would be like playing a game without having any rules. What a chaotic mess that would be. The game would likely go nowhere and efforts to play it would probably end in frustration and anger.

So it is with our interactions with others and with our self. Our children need boundaries and limits. So do the adults with whom we interact. And we often need to set limits with our self. How often have you taken on more work than you should have or wanted to? How often have you said "yes" when you really wanted to say "no"? Have you ever overspent? Overeaten? Overelaborated? Overgiven? Overimbibed? Do you ever disregard time? Disregard your physical needs? Disregard your emotional needs? Disregard the limits set by others relative to what they need and want from you?

All of these are daily, momentary ways that the need for boundary setting enters our lives. We are given many opportunities to practice setting and keeping limits that help us to be healthy and strong individuals, individuals who are then more capable of healthy relationships.

But setting limits does not come easily for many of us. Some of us have no practice in it at all. We have never even thought of the idea of setting a limit. Others of us think we have set boundaries but really have just been trying to manage and control the behaviors of others. Our limit setting has been focused on what we think others need their lives to be like rather than on what limits we need to set for our own lives.

And even once we know what boundaries we need to set, stating them is hard. All sorts of fears arise, including fears that the other person will not tolerate the limits and leave, or fears that we are just wrong to take the stand that we think is right for us.

And then our task is to stick with the limit we have set. Setting boundaries and then not following through with them greatly undermines our efforts to establish our self. When we set a limit with someone and then don't stick with it, the other person learns to not take us seriously. He or she knows that we really aren't going to do anything if he or she doesn't respect our limits, and so the chaotic game continues and frustration and anger mount.

Setting boundaries for our self and with others is important and can be difficult. The ideas in this section on Setting Healthy Boundaries include some of the basics of how to set limits. The ideas are all directed at helping you to listen to your self more carefully and fully, and to successfully communicate to your self and to others what you will and won't accept, what you will and won't do. The ideas are directed at helping you to find and to keep your center as you assert and enforce your boundaries.

## SETTING HEALTHY BOUNDARIES
# Slow Down

It is so easy to simply react when we are angry, anxious, confused, disappointed. We want to impulsively blurt out our feelings and thoughts without thinking. And we do.

In order to disentangle, however, we need to slow this process way down. We want to move from reacting to acting.

And in order to act, we need to have our self centered and aware of what is being said and what we want to say back.

So when you're in an interaction with someone and feel your self start to lose your balance, slow down your reactions; create some time and space between what the person says to you and how you respond back.

There's a lot of truth to the old adage of counting to ten when we are upset. Now, rushing from count one to count ten in order to go ahead and blurt out your slightly delayed response is not what I have in mind.

What I do have in mind is mindfully bringing your focus to your breath and following that for several counts. (I will speak more about this in the section on Developing Spirituality.) Perhaps ten slow breaths would be good. And while you are doing that, keep your focus on your breath, not on what you are just dying to say to the other person.

The object here is to take a momentary break so that you can collect your self. That includes your thoughts and feelings, needs and wants.

We are slowing down the interactions here so that the communications you make are not out of habit, impulse, or reaction. Rather, this slowing down increases the chances that you will more effectively communicate what you mean. You will keep your feeling of centeredness and not have to run around apologizing and explaining your self for days.

When I am centered and in good form, I can sometimes anticipate moments in interactions with others that stand to upset me or at least disturb me. When I anticipate this, I consciously tell my self to not respond right away to what the other might say to me. I tell my self to simply listen to him or her, hear him or her out, and then intentionally pause and calm my self before I proceed.

Sometimes in a situation like this, I can't proceed until I actually take a break from the interaction. For me this may mean taking a walk outside or going to another room for a while. For others, a break may be journaling, talking to a friend, reading, or any number of pleasurable outlets that refresh us and help us to figure out how we do want to respond to what has been said or done to us.

And it is okay to take this type of break. Generally we don't have to give the other person a response right away. We may feel like we have to or want to, but often we don't have to. So take the time you need to respond in the way that best represents you.

Whether we slow down our interactions by minutes or hours or even days, the point is that in order to speak for our true self, we need to make sure that we are not caught in the tentacles of a bad interaction. When we are caught in this way, we are on the defense and struggle to free our self in random and aggressive ways. We even send out our own tentacles to entrap the other.

Slowing down our reactions enables us to slide out of the way of the tentacles, leaving us free to clarify what we truly want to say and to assert it in a way that is respectful of both the other and our self.

SETTING HEALTHY BOUNDARIES

# Listen to You

It is so easy to narrow our focus onto the other person when we are angry, anxious, confused, or disappointed. As an interaction becomes more intense, those of us who are prone to entanglements become increasingly riveted on what the other person is saying, how he or she looks, and what he or she is doing. We lose our self in this way.

When we are completely absorbed with listening to the other person, we cannot also listen to our self. In order to disentangle, we need to bring our focus back onto our self. This is the heart of my message here. So, in the space we create for our self by slowing down, we need to listen to the voices within us that can help us know how we want to respond. Those voices include at least the voices of our minds, our hearts, our bodies, and our spirit.

The voice of our mind can tell us what we think about this situation. It can tell us what is logical, fair, appropriate, and acceptable to us. Our mind reminds us of our position relative to this situation, which perhaps we quickly lost track of as the interaction took off. Our mind can help us sort through the variables involved, organize and evaluate those variables, and plan some course of action.

But to hear only the voice of your mind will not give you full data about your self. The voice of your heart is also important to listen to and factor in. By the voice of your heart, I mean your emotions and feelings. How do you feel about this situation? About this person involved in this interaction? How do you feel about how you are treated? About how you treat your self relative to this person and situation? Are you okay with things as they are? Do you need something to be different? How do you feel even asking your self these questions?

The voice of your body has many important messages for you as well. By voice of your body, I mean your physical self. How do you feel physically? Are you aware of stress, tension, chronic pain, or illness? Do you have physical complaints that you ignore? How does your body feel when you are caught in an entanglement? What does it do? Does your body move toward the problem or away from it, or is it paralyzed? Many years ago I read a suggestion that has been meaningful to me and applies here: When you can't figure out what you think or feel, notice what your body is doing. Our physical self has a lot of important information for us.

And the voice of our spirit is equally important to hear, though too often it is forgotten or disregarded as we forge ahead into our entanglements. The voice of the spirit is the opposite of our forcing solutions. The voice of the spirit may be our gut feelings, our intuitions that are strong and clear and yet may defy clear explanations. The voice of our spirit may be through our contact with a power greater than our self, a contact in which we let go of our tight hold of a situation and allow things to unfold on their own. The voice of our spirit may be through our own quiet mindfulness that rests the mind and heart and allows pieces to come together in ways we could never imagine or create on our own.

Listening to our self involves hearing *all* of these voices and not jumping to conclusions or actions based on none or one or two of our voices. If we don't listen to all of them, we are not being fair to our self. We are making perhaps important decisions based on inadequate information.

Granted, as we listen to these voices, we may find that there is some conflict among them. Logic may tell you to leave while your heart says to stay. Everything may be working out well for you in your relationship, but something tells you it's wrong to be in this relationship. As we listen to these conflicting messages, we need to respect them all and weigh them against each other as best we can so as to figure out where we stand at that moment and what we need to say or do, if anything, right then. Maybe all we can say at that time is that we are confused and we'll have to get back to the other person when we have more to say.

It is amazing how much information about our self is right here with us all along. We just have to make sure that we tune in. If the channel is fuzzy at first, please don't just change the dial. Simply adjust the antenna until the picture is clearer and then pay good attention.

SETTING HEALTHY BOUNDARIES

# Use "I" Statements

It is so easy to start pointing our finger at the other person when we are angry, anxious, confused, or disappointed. In a heated situation, often one of the first words out of our mouth is "you":

"You never do what you say you're going to do!"

"You do the same thing and more of it!"

"You have a problem and just don't want to face it!"

"You are a jerk."

"You make me sick."

"You're the one who got us in this situation."

"You're always _____."

"You're never _____."

Starting statements with "you" generally puts the other person on the defensive *immediately*. When someone says "You . . ." to me, my response is to account for my self, to explain my self, to defend my self. I'm now ready to talk/argue about this statement about me rather than address whatever topic we were trying to discuss.

"You" statements feel very personal and solicit very personal responses. Personal responses often are loaded with emotion and have an extremely narrowed focus. Our focus becomes that of protecting our self against what feels like an assault on us and may well be. We need to defend our very self that is feeling bombarded.

In order to disentangle, I find it much more useful to start statements with "I" when I am engaged in an intense and conflicted interaction:

"I am disappointed that you have changed your mind."

"I am angry that this work did not get taken care of."

"I am not happy living in this situation. I need to make some changes for myself."

"I don't know what to say right now. I am confused and very angry. I'll get back with you later."

"I am worried about you. I miss how it used to be with us."

"I really wish you would go there with me."

Starting statements with "I" helps to create a climate where we may be able to continue to discuss things. "I" statements do not put the other person on the defense. They are simply clear statements to the other person of what's going on with you and where you stand.

To this end, this is why "I" statements contribute to disentangling. In order to make an "I" statement, you have to stop and think about how you are feeling and what you do want. Sometimes this is a real challenge. As these intense and unproductive interchanges progress, we get further and further from the original point. "I" statements help us to anchor our self back in what we wanted to say in the first place.

Similarly, "I" statements reduce entanglements because they are not putting the other person on the defensive. We are not sending out our tentacles to snare and entrap the other person. Doing so only intensifies the argument and greatly reduces the chances that anything will be gained by it. "I" statements to the other person offer them clear information about you. They can have a steadying impact on the conversation at hand.

I find "I" statements to be helpful for me. They help me to re-center my self and to not make a difficult situation even worse. And often, I find that "I" statements help me to start finding the path out of an entangled interaction.

SETTING HEALTHY BOUNDARIES

# Make Statements Rather Than Ask Questions

Questions can be okay. And they can be a problem if we are asking them so as to manipulate or control the other person or situation:

"Have you asked for time off from work yet?"

"Do you know when you are going to ask?"

"Have you even thought of how you're going to do it?"

"You are going to ask, aren't you?"

---

"Have you finished that report yet?"

"When do you plan on doing it?"

"Don't you think you should stay home tonight and work on it?"

"Aren't you worried about getting it done?"

These sets of questions are examples of how we get on a roll in trying to get another person to do what we think he or she should be doing.

The effect of such questioning is profound.

The person being questioned feels attacked and needs to account for or defend his or her self. Notice the number of times "you" appears in those questions. Whether "you" is used in statements or questions, the result is essentially the same: The other person is on guard and the chances of effective communication are pretty much shot.

The person asking the questions generally is not having a very good time of it, either. By our questions, we are usually seeking some specific answer. And this type of "questioning" usually does not produce that answer. So we get more and more frustrated and ask more and more questions. And we get angry and lost.

If we really stop and think about what we want to say to the other person by all of these questions, we can usually make a statement that conveys what we are really feeling and want behind this wall of questions:

> "I am really hoping we can go on the trip we are planning."

> "I'll be glad when you know if you can get off from work for that time."

> "The sooner you can find out, the better it will be for me and the other arrangements I need to make for the trip."

> "Please let me know as soon as you find out about getting time off."

---

> "I'm worried that you are not going to get your report done on time."

> "If you need something from me that will help you get going on it, let me know."

These statements more clearly express where I stand and what's going on with me relative to the other person. The statements help both of us to know what we are trying to say rather than dragging the other person around with questions that have implied meanings and hints.

Statements to the other person give us a foundation upon which we stand. That foundation is built on our clarity of thoughts and our emotional centeredness, which come from asking our self questions about how we feel and what we want, and then taking those answers and expressing them as statements to the other person.

SETTING HEALTHY BOUNDARIES

# Set and State Your Boundaries

This disentangling idea involves two steps: setting and stating boundaries. Don't try to do them at the same time. Don't state your boundaries out loud as you are figuring them out. They just may not be what you really mean and want:

"If you don't ask for that time off today, I'm divorcing you."

---

"If you don't complete your report tonight, I'm selling your car."

Instead, first decide for your self what your boundaries are. Using your skills of slowing down and listening to you, you can figure out:

* what you will and won't accept from the other person;
* what you will and won't do for him or her;
* what you can and cannot offer him or her;
* what your limitations are in terms of time, money, and energy;
* how much you can physically and emotionally invest in the situation;
* what would be the best for you in this situation.

These are not necessarily easy questions. Often we don't know the answers immediately.

So how do we find those answers if they don't come to us right away?

Well, while we are considering what the other person has asked of us, we look at our schedule, we check on our finances, we consider what we have on our own list of what we need to do.

While we are thinking about what the other person said or did to us, we need to notice how we are feeling, what we are needing, and what we are doing.

We need to take all the time we need to set our boundaries.

We need to make sure our boundaries feel right to us.

And once we have figured out our boundaries and are comfortable with them, we need to let the other person know what they are. We need to state them simply and with ownership:

> "I cannot go on the trip if I don't know your plans by Friday."

> "I will not call for our reservations until you tell me when you can get off from work."

> "I am going to make my own reservation for my flight. I'm leaving it up to you to make your own once you know your work schedule."

---

> "I need to work on the computer tonight for a couple of hours starting around 9:00 p.m. I just wanted you to know so you can plan your work on your report around that."

> "I've asked you enough about your report. I'm not going to bring it up again. It's up to you to take care of it."

Easy said? Easy done? No. Boundary setting is not easily done by many of us. It is hard to set our boundaries and often even harder to state them to others, and still harder to stick with them. Many of our people-pleasing, conflict-avoiding behaviors come right to the front and center stage at this point when we are trying to set limits with others.

We are so afraid of upsetting, inconveniencing, disappointing, and / or angering others that we only reluctantly approach boundary setting. Guilt gladly steps in to make our assertive behaviors even more difficult, if not impossible at times.

So with these personal obstacles in mind, the following additional ideas about Setting Healthy Boundaries are offered to help us maintain our strength, clarity, and centeredness as we present our boundaries to others.

SETTING HEALTHY BOUNDARIES
# Stick with Your Limits

It is so easy not to follow through with the boundaries we set. When we state them, we may feel strong and sure. Give us a few minutes, hours, or days, and we're either backing down from what we said or pretending that we never set a new boundary.

It is no wonder that we have trouble sticking with our limits. A quick glance back at the characteristics of adult children of alcoholics described by Janet Woititz (see Appendix A) will remind us of a least some of the reasons:

* Our fears of abandonment allow us to believe that if we stick by our limit with another person, he or she may leave us.

* Our needs for constant approval and affirmation are often thwarted by limit setting as the person we are setting the limits with often is not approving of our new decisions.

* Our super-responsibility may have us believing that if we follow through with this limit, whatever we believe needs to be taken care of may not get done, and so we need to go ahead and do it anyway.

* Our loyalty may instill in us the belief that we are not really being fair to the other person and that we need to stick by him or her in our same old ways.

* Our needs for immediate gratification are also thwarted. Though the limit setting we are doing may in the long run really improve our situation, at first it may not bring the gratifying results we are looking for. In fact, it may leave the limit-setter feeling even worse than before.

And then there is plain old guilt. We may feel guilty because we are "doing this to him or her." We feel bad about saying "no." We feel bad about looking after our needs. Guilt moves in like a weight upon our chest and heart. And it sings its song in our ear. Guilt makes it hard to stick with our limits.

In order to disentangle, we need to stick with the boundaries we have set. If we don't, we stand to just continue with the tangled games in which we are caught.

We will be giving the message that we really don't mean what we say.

We will be telling the other person that, though we were upset at the time, we can get over it and accept things as they usually are.

We are saying that we really don't respect our self enough to enforce what we have decided we need.

At our worst, we can go back and apologize for the boundaries we set, ask that the other person forget about them, and then try to make up to the other person. This really encourages the old tangled ways.

And my experience is that I feel pretty horrible again fairly quickly after I discard and/or discount my boundaries.

So how to stick with them? Use your self-talk. Keep reminding your self of how and for what reasons you set these limits. Be a broken record, and keep repeating your boundaries if they are being challenged. Remind your self of what probably is going to happen if you don't stick with your limits. Remind your self of how miserable you will feel if these new limits are not enforced. Remind your self that people notice when you do not do what you say. Remind your self that this is what you need to do for you and that it's okay to make a decision like this with your self in mind.

You may have to learn to sit with your guilt a bit. It is not going to automatically go away with these reminders. And you may have to sit with the discomfort that comes from the disapproval you are receiving and the conflict that you are experiencing.

In order to make real changes that untangle us, we need to go through these uncomfortable feelings that come from doing things differently and believe that our stating and sticking with our limits can help us to eventually be involved in healthier ways with others. And we can, sooner or later, feel better, too.

SETTING HEALTHY BOUNDARIES
# Say Things Once

There's a lot to be said for brevity.

Saying what we need to say and then stopping has real strength and cleanliness. It conveys that we know what we are talking about and are sure of it. It can also have some matter-of-factness to it that says, "I'm not making a big deal over this. This is just where I stand."

Saying things once can be hard. We tend instead to repeat our self in a variety of ways and for a variety of reasons.

We repeat our self by bringing the topic up again and again. We repeat our self by explaining further and further what we mean and why we are doing what we are doing. We are repeating our self every time we say to the other, "Do you understand why I am doing this? Do you understand what I am saying?" And we repeat our self when we decide that we have not made our self clear to the other person and need to say the same thing in twelve different ways.

So why all of this repeating? Another glance at Janet Woititz's characteristics of adult children of alcoholics gives us lots of possible reasons. We are uncomfortable with the change that our new boundaries will likely bring. We are afraid the other person will leave us. We don't like the disapproval we may be receiving. We are starting to feel responsible for this whole mess.

And so we overstate our case, hoping that the other person will come to some understanding of what we are saying and doing and be able to say to us, "I understand exactly what you mean, and I think you are doing exactly the right thing by setting this limit with me. I love you dearly for doing it, and I will never leave you."

But repeating our self is not likely to produce such results. In fact, going over and over a topic often antagonizes and angers both parties and confuses and dilutes the original point.

So once we are ready and able to state our boundaries with someone else, I find it useful to try to say them once. Granted, sometimes clarification may be needed. But after that, I need to pay careful attention to any impulses I may have to say more about this limit I am setting. Usually those impulses are coming from my own insecurities about the situation. And I am learning that continuing to repeat and explain my self in these situations is not going to alleviate my insecurities.

I need to work with and work through my insecurities in my own ways, separate from this necessary boundary setting with someone else.

In this present moment, I just need to state my limits with the other person and then stop talking about it.

SETTING HEALTHY BOUNDARIES

# Say Things Cleanly and without Extensive Discussion

This suggestion is a variation of "say things once," and I don't have a lot to say about it.

Saying things cleanly means making "I" statements that are concise and to the point. These statements clearly reflect what it is you are trying to convey to the other about how you feel and what you want or need. These statements are not muddied by hints, old issues, or accusations.

Saying things without extensive discussion means just what it says. Some discussion may be necessary in order to have effective and fair communication. But beware of extensive discussion. Extensive discussion can easily get us away from our point and away from our center. As we elaborate on our boundaries or as we answer questions and explain our self to the other person, it is so easy to lose track of what we were first saying and meaning.

It is so easy to slip into unclear communication that rambles on and on from one unhappy topic to another. It is especially easy for this to happen when we are upset and are trying to say things that are difficult for us to say, such as setting boundaries.

And we will slip into these tangled moments despite our best efforts sometimes. But be reassured we can find our way out.

Take a deep breath and simply return your focus to you. Remind your self of what you want to say to the other person, offer it to them in an "I" statement, and leave it at that.

SETTING HEALTHY BOUNDARIES

# Stick to the Topic

It is so easy to get off the immediate topic when we are upset. In our fury, we add on this and that, escalating the argument and losing the original point. As we get more and more lost and angry, we pull in more and more old stuff that still makes us mad and/or causes us pain.

Returning to one of the examples we worked with earlier in this section on boundaries, here is what may be to you an all-too-familiar demonstration of us getting off the topic:

Susan: "Have you asked for time off from work yet?"

David: "No."

Susan: "When do you plan on asking?"

David: "I don't know."

Susan: "What do you mean, 'I don't know'?"

David: "Nothing in particular. I don't know."

Susan: "You make me so mad. You never give me a straight answer when I ask you a question."

David: "Well, you ask too many questions. I'm tired of all your questions. I feel like I'm being cross-examined."

Susan: "Well, somebody needs to cross-examine you. Anybody who could put off asking for his vacation days needs his head examined. What's wrong with you?"

David: "There's nothing wrong with me. You seem to be the one having the problem."

Susan: "I'm not the one with the problem. I'm not the one who put things off and screwed up our vacation last time."

David: "Yeah, and I'm not the one who made such a scene in the restaurant that our children refuse to eat out with us anymore."

Susan: "That wouldn't have happened if you had just answered my question then about the checkbook."

David: "You and that damn checkbook. You act like the world's going to fall apart if everything isn't just right in it."

Susan: "And you act like you don't care if we have a penny in it. You're terrible with money!"

This argument could go on and on. And it does go on and on if we do not intervene on our own behalf. We can get on this angry roll and stuff just keeps coming out of our mouth.

And the original question about the vacation plans is lost. And who wants to go on a vacation at this point anyway?

Intervening on our own behalf is an important notion to remind our self of in this type of situation. We need to be vigilant of our own impulses to insert another issue into this discussion, and we need to be aware of invitations from the other person to change the subject as well. Often we are both parties in this changing of subjects.

When topics are added on like this, it makes it next to impossible to talk about and resolve any of the issues. They become very piled up and tangled, and without sorting through them carefully and handling them topic by topic, we are not able to resolve them. Granted, some of the topics may be interrelated and need to be considered in this way, but here I am speaking of us loading on topics in angry, accusing ways that avoid dealing with the topic at hand.

So we need to be prepared to intervene on our own behalf when the conversation is starting to get muddied. We need to be aware when we are slipping away from the original topic. We need to be aware of how we are feeling as we get further into this unproductive argument. We need to be ready to bring our self back to our original question or statement. And we need to be ready to repeatedly return to it if necessary.

If we are making such efforts to intervene on our own behalf, the above argument may look something like this:

Susan: "Have you asked for time off from work yet?"

David: "No."

Susan: "When do you plan on asking?"

David: "I don't know."

Susan: "What do you mean, 'I don't know'?"

David: "Nothing in particular. I don't know."

Susan: "You make me so mad. You never give me a straight answer when I ask you a question."

David: "Well, you ask too many questions. I'm tired of all your questions. I feel like I'm being cross-examined."

Susan: (*Pausing. Breathing. Listening to self.*) "Okay. I hear you. What I mean to say is that I'm really looking forward to going with you on this trip. In order to get the tickets at the discounted price, I need to make the reservations by Friday."

David: "So, why didn't you tell me this before? I never feel like I'm getting clear information from you."

Susan: (*Pausing. Breathing. Listening to self.*) "I'm sure I told you about this deadline when we first talked about this trip. I haven't mentioned it since because I thought you knew."

David: "You make too many assumptions."

Susan: (*Pausing. Breathing. Listening to self.*) "What I am saying now is that I need to know your vacation schedule before Friday in order to get our discounted tickets."

David: "There you go with the money stuff again. I don't think these tickets you are getting are at such a good price anyway!"

Susan: (*Pausing. Breathing. Listening to self.*) "Well, I'm calling for my reservations on Friday. If you can go and want me to make your reservations too, let me know. I need to go now."

Again, this is easier said than done. Sticking to the topic can be a real challenge. And it can be a useful thing to do in order to untangle our self and whatever is being discussed. By returning to the topic at hand, we can work with that issue until it has a level of clarity and/or resolution that then frees us to move on to the next and perhaps equally important topic.

# Stay in the Present

Many books have been written on this topic over many years. Living in the present is a concept central to Eastern philosophy and religion. Mindfulness is another word used to describe this act of being in the present moment. *Wherever You Go, There You Are* written by Jon Kabat-Zinn and *The Miracle of Mindfulness* by Thich Nhat Hanh are two books that offer wonderful details about this practice of mindfulness.

For our purposes here, I will be making simple statements about how being in the present or mindfulness can be useful to us in our efforts to disentangle. In the next section of this book, *Developing Spirituality*, many of the ideas I describe reflect the writings in the above two books and will help you with your cultivation of mindfulness.

For now, I simply want to comment on the value of being in the present when we are communicating with someone else and perhaps setting boundaries with him or her.

It is so easy to jump to the future or return to the past when we are entangled. Entanglements have us off center. We may be worried, upset, confused, or angry. And our mind interacts with our feelings and creates more turmoil.

Our thoughts rush to the catastrophic things that may happen in the future if we set and stick with our boundaries: The other may leave me; I will be financially ruined; I will have to be alone; I will never find someone else; and on and on.

Or our thoughts go back to the past, fueling the present fires more than is useful in the present moment: We think of other things the person has done in the past that are different from what we are talking about but that also irritate us; we start to predict the other's present and future behavior based on how he or she has responded in the past, failing to allow that perhaps something may be different this time if we are present to it.

So as we interact with the other person, our mind may be busily chatting away about any or all of these past and future things, as well as about the things we know we want to get across to the other person.

And these are all obstacles to being in the present moment.

Being in the present moment involves quieting these thoughts and bringing your focus to the moment-to-moment interactions you are presently having with this person. It involves being aware of your body, your thoughts, your feelings, and your actions right now.

It is quite interesting how many of the common expressions we use describe or refer to this de-centering of our self that comes from not being in the present.

One expression I have come to understand better and like is "I was beside my self!" I have heard this expression used to describe how angry or upset a person was in a particular situation. What this expression means to me is that in that moment, a person is not centered, is not with his or her self. The person feels ripped and torn by his emotions and like he is losing touch with his body, mind, and spirit. The person literally feels like he is beside his self and not *with* his self. He is not mindful with what is going on with him at that time.

As another common expression says, "I fell to pieces." And, of course, the antidote offered to someone who describes her self this way is "Well, get your self together." Exactly!

A third expression that relates to this being in the present is "having the presence of mind." A friend helped me to see this one day as I told him a brief story from my day about how I had kept my self from creating an angry and unfortunate situation with my daughter.

She and I were supposed to go to a friend's birthday party. I knew I could not pick her up for the party until very close to the time we were expected there. I had asked her to be ready and told her we would have to leave right away.

In my oh-too-usual rushing style, I arrived at our house in my hurry-up-let's-go mode, in large part because I was running, as usual, very close to late. As I got out of the car, my daughter greeted me with happiness and pleasure. She wanted me to come in and see what she had created as gifts and decorations for this friend. She was so tickled with her work.

In that rushing moment, I could have lost it and said, "No! Let's go. I told you to be ready." But as my friend later described to me, I had the presence of mind to slow my self down, really notice her and her happiness, become aware that I did not want to mess up what she was enjoying, and realize that she was only asking for two minutes of our time.

So I caught my self, joined her, and enjoyed her pleasure and delight, and then we both left for the party calmly and with good feelings.

Being in the present moment requires that we slow down, get out of our heads, and tune in—tune in to now, tune in to what we are experiencing and to what is being said to us and is happening around us in that moment.

So when we are having a heavy-duty conversation or are about to have one, we need to be with our self and remind our self that what is being said is about now and is not a predictor of things to come or an indictment for things past.

In its healthiest form, what is being said now is about now and is best experienced and taken as that.

SETTING HEALTHY BOUNDARIES

# Listen to the Other Person

The suggestion here is to listen to the other person without losing our self to what we are hearing.

It is important to be able to listen to the other person and to truly hear what the person is saying to us. The more we can accurately hear what the other person is saying, the more likely we are to be dealing with reality and not illusions.

It is important to be able to listen to the other person without losing track of what we are trying to say, without getting upset and flying off the handle, and without changing our point of view to the other's when we really don't want to.

So how do we do all of this at once? We do it with lots of self-awareness and conscious efforts to center and re-center our self as we are talking.

The following list offers some specific suggestions that we can use to help us with this centered, effective listening:

* Slow down the pace of your conversation.
* Make eye contact with the other person.

* Pay attention to *what* the other person is saying, as well as to *how* he or she is saying it.

* Notice if *what* is being said matches *how* the person is saying it. Are you hearing one message, or are you getting two different messages between the person's verbal and nonverbal communications?

* Seek clarification. Feel free to say, "I don't understand."

* Use "I" statements.

* Inquire as to whether you have heard the person correctly. Tentatively repeat back what you think you are hearing from him or her.

* Don't try to tell the other person what he or she means or how he or she feels.

* Welcome any clarifications to you if you have heard the other person wrong.

* Then, repeat back to the person what you now are hearing from him or her.

The only assignment for our self here is to listen. We are trying to really understand what the other person is saying to us. We do not have to do anything more in this moment. We don't have to give the person a final answer, make a decision, or conclude anything right now.

As we are listening, we may be having a variety of internal reactions, from surprise and relief to outright frustration. Whatever we may be experiencing, it is useful to be aware of those feelings and useful to sit with them for a while along with what we are hearing from the other person.

And then, as we sort through all of this information about our self and the other, the answers will come.

For the present, just listen.

SETTING HEALTHY BOUNDARIES
# Be Careful of Defending, Justifying, and Convincing

As we listen to someone talk to us, we are commonly going to have emotional reactions to what the person is saying. Perhaps we are pleased or excited. We may disagree or even be angered. Or perhaps we are confused and are not sure what the other person is trying to say to us.

If I am confused, I find it useful to say so and to ask for clarification using some of the suggestions in the previous section on listening. Let the person know what you think he or she is saying, and if the person says that it is not what he or she means and offers more information, then again let the person know what you are hearing him or her say.

When we let the other person know what we hear him or her saying, this helps us also to slow our self down and clarify to our self what he or she is saying. This can be very centering for us, as often in this type of conflicted conversation we are slipping further away from our center as we try to get our points across. Repeating out loud what the other person is saying helps to ensure that we are working toward communicating and not arguing.

When we are clear about what the other person is saying to us, it is useful to acknowledge what we are hearing, and it is important to try to stop at that for the present moment.

It is so easy, instead, to defend, rationalize, explain, justify, or convince in response to what the other person is saying. It seems to be almost a natural instinct to respond in these ways that protect our self. My experience, however, is that if I respond in these ways too quickly, I can lose my centeredness.

I become reactive to the situation and to what is being said. I slip into trying to control someone else's reactions and opinions. I want to set things straight right then. I want to make things right immediately. So I become attached to these goals in an unhealthy way and lose track of what my original point was. And in so doing, I lose track of my self.

And I start to feel off-center. My thoughts become less clear, my behavior more agitated, my tone harsh or insecure, maybe even submissive.

If we are not careful, defending, justifying, and convincing can slip us into reactions rather than the conscious actions we want to be taking. We do want to be able to respond to what the other person is saying and even to defend our self if we need to.

What we don't want to do is to jump to these behaviors if we are upset and off-center. Doing so only increases the chances that we will remain entangled and perhaps tighten the web around our self a bit more, leaving us feeling worse than when we began.

So, go slowly. Listen. Seek clarification. Acknowledge what you hear. And then sit with your self and this information, and consciously decide what you want to say or do in response.

SETTING HEALTHY BOUNDARIES

# Be Conscious and Observing of Your Self

As we get involved more and more in an entanglement, we lose touch with our self. We are so caught up in things outside of our self: what the other person is saying or doing, our fears about the future, defending our self in the present, what other people will think.

As we become more and more attached to these things outside of our self, we lose contact with our self. Not only do we get distracted from our original point, we also lose touch with what we are saying and how we are saying it. These are the moments when we say those terrible things that we regret later or at least wish we had not said. We are not aware of our tone of voice or our nonverbal behaviors. Our actions may become impulsive and without thought or awareness.

We have no "presence of mind."

We are "beside our self," not with our self.

In order to achieve and maintain our centeredness, it is important to work toward staying with our self.

This means that although we may be very upset, we stay aware of those feelings and develop our ability to actually observe them as we are experiencing them.

This observing is not to be confused with dissociative experiences where people report that they are outside of their body watching themselves. In those experiences, people usually are feeling unattached to their self. It is like they are observing someone separate from their self, and they have no power or influence over what is happening.

Here I am speaking of observing the self in a way that is not separate but rather is consciously taking ownership of who we are, what we are experiencing, and what we are saying and doing.

This conscious observing of our self as we are interacting with another person means that we are at least as aware of our self as we are of things outside of our self.

Usually when we start to lose track of our self, we feel off-center and generally bothered and upset. Sometimes we feel quite lost. In these moments, we want to be aware of how we are feeling and what we are experiencing. This awareness can be a useful step that can help us to come back to more solid ground.

So if I am yelling angry things at someone, I want to simultaneously be observing my self do that. I want to see that "Oh, here I am, yelling and saying these things. Is this what I want to be doing? Is this what I want to be saying?" I want to be aware of my tone, my actions, my physical reactions.

Or, if I am saying "yes" to something when I really want to say "no," I want to be aware that I am doing this and notice what is going on with me as I do this. I want to see that "Oh, here I am, agreeing to do this when it really is a problem for me. I'm not feeling happy about this. I am even feeling angry that this person has asked me to do this again."

Conscious ownership of our self can help us to not make difficult situations worse. It can even help us to make difficult situations better for our self. It provides us with an anchor in a storm. It can help us to feel more in control of our self. It can help us to say and do what we really want to convey. It can help us to have fewer regrets and entanglements.

SETTING HEALTHY BOUNDARIES
# Learn When to Stop

There is definitely an art to knowing when to stop.

Stopping at the right time greatly increases the chances of our keeping our center and perhaps making our point, and generally improves the quality of the communication we are having.

But knowing when to stop can be a true challenge. We get on a roll and don't want to stop. We keep repeating our self because "we are not finished." We keep saying the same thing over and over in a variety of ways, hoping that this new approach will help the other person to see our point and perhaps concede. We leave the discussion and still come back to say more that has come to our mind. And even if the other person does concede in some way, we then go on and on about why he or she should have done this a long time ago; what's wrong with him or her that he or she could not see this before; and blah, blah, blah.

And so, as they say, we "beat it to death." And, in the process, we beat our self and the relationship to death as well. Good spirit goes out the door. Antagonism and defensiveness take over as a matter of course.

And so, what is this art of knowing when to stop?

Knowing when to stop involves being with our self during the interaction and thus being aware of when we have said all we need to say for now. It involves recognizing when we may be starting to lose our center. Hints of that may be our increasing defensiveness or efforts to convince, increasing feelings of agitation or irritation, or accusations about topics other than the present one.

Knowing when to stop also involves noticing what is happening outside of our self as well: How is the other person responding? Are we having a conversation or an argument? Does it feel safe to continue right now?

Knowing when to stop involves being conscious of all of this data in the moment and then intervening on our own behalf.

When we start feeling like we need to stop, that is probably a very good moment to stop. And it can be as simple as saying to your self and to the other person, "I need to stop for right now."

SETTING HEALTHY BOUNDARIES

# Stop

The art of stopping involves knowing when to stop and then actually stopping.

And, as with other ideas for disentangling, this is often more easily said than done.

It is hard to stop our self when we are on a roll. It is sort of like trying to stop a sled when you're part way down the hill headed for a tree. But if we don't stop the sled, we know what's coming.

So it can be with our discussions with someone else. We may not be headed for a tree, necessarily, but we may be at least headed for a ditch or some obstacle if we continue on this path.

Let's remind our self of the need to stop this roll we are on and avoid the unnecessary consequences of continuing it.

We can save our self and the interaction if we say what we want to say, talk about it with centeredness, tune into when is a good time to stop, and then stop.

Enough said.

SETTING HEALTHY BOUNDARIES

# Boundaries and You

**Think of someone with whom you want to set a limit or boundary. Perhaps you need to say "no" to something. Perhaps you want to stop doing something you have done in the past. Perhaps you need to stop accepting an unacceptable behavior from someone else. Slow down and take whatever time you need to think about this:**

What do you want, need, feel?

What is the boundary you need to set?

What exactly do you want to say to the other person?

What is an "I" statement that will
convey your message?


**Now think about actually telling the other person about this limit. What are things within you that you need to be aware of in order not to lose your center as you set this limit?**

Do you tend to go on and on?
Do you get defensive? Accusatory? Mean?

Do you apologize for having a limit and try to make
the other person okay with what you are saying?

Do you tend to bring up unfinished stuff from
the past? Or generalize to the future?

What else is true for you?

**And now think of tools that could help you
to state your limits and not lose your self.
What would it be like if you:**

First took a deep breath and brought your
self fully into the present moment?

Made sure that you paid as much attention to your
self in the interaction as to the other person?

Listened to the other person without losing track
of you and the point you needed to make?

Resisted your impulses to react and took a mental
and/or physical break from the interaction if you were
feeling confused, upset, or generally off-center?

Stopped when your good judgment told you to stop?

**Now, with all of this information, decide
what you want to do about setting this
boundary and how you are going to do it.**

What do you want to say?

What are things about your self you want to be
particularly aware of that can lead to further
entanglements in this type of situation?

What are tools you are going to try to use to increase
the chances of this being a healthy communication
that respects you and the other person?

"There's nothing else I can do.
I have to let go."

*Lindsey, age 19*

# Developing Spirituality

The process of disentangling would be scary and empty if it did not also involve spiritual growth in our lives. Its presence is important as we work to apply all of the previous ideas on disentangling.

Facing illusions involves changes, letting go of hopes and ideas to which we have been attached. This letting go involves a grieving process and a leap of faith. The leap of faith involves our spirituality. Spirituality stabilizes us and reminds us that we are not the ultimate power in charge here. That reminder helps us to tell our self that maybe what we think we want is not really what is best for us and that our letting go of things we cannot control enables things to unfold in the way they are meant to develop.

Detaching from someone else or something involves emotional distance and subsequent changes in our behaviors. We often stop doing things for others that we have normally done, and we stop some of our own reactive behaviors that have kept the entanglements alive and sick. Making these changes in our lives is also greatly helped by spirituality. It can be scary to move away from the other person in these ways. Our feelings of abandonment, guilt, and fear can turn us quickly around and have us doing the same old things and thus feeding the loss of our self in another. Again, spirituality backs us up, supports us, catches us. Spirituality is our comfort, our place of rest, reassurance, and good company. It is the source of the serenity that we seek.

Setting boundaries also involves changes. Setting boundaries is about doing things differently than in the past, and it is about us becoming different people by virtue of our setting these limits. Many of us have not previously been good at saying and enforcing what we will and won't accept from others. When we start doing this, everything may start changing. And this is where spirituality comes in. Once again, spirituality offers us help in strengthening the self we are creating. When we are in touch with our power greater than our self, we can better figure out what boundaries are best for us and gather support as we work to stick with those limits. Spirituality can help us keep our center when we are feeling quite drawn away from it.

So what do I mean by spirituality?

Spirituality here is personal to you.

In general, I am talking about the concept of a power greater than your self, a concept central to twelve-step programs. This is the belief that we are not the ultimate power in our lives. It is a belief that we are not in full control of everything. It is not an abdication of responsibility. We certainly do need to take responsibility for our self, *and* we need to be able to see and willing to accept when things are not in our control, and turn them over to this greater power.

Specifically, this notion of a greater power is for you to determine. For people with religious beliefs, this greater power will most likely be the God of their faith. For others, this greater power may be in nature, in their friends, in silence, in something they love. It could be in any number of things that

I could not begin to think of here. And for others, spirituality may not be anything particularly tangible or visualized but rather a feeling, an experience that defies easy descriptions. And for even others, this notion of spirituality is so distant and perhaps even foreign that they have only a glimmer of what this might mean and feel like or they have little to no interest or belief in it at all.

Whatever your source of spirituality and however well it may or may not be developed, I have found that the following ideas help me to access my higher power and strengthen my spirituality. In so doing, I feel much more centered. Whether I am facing my illusions, detaching, or setting boundaries, spirituality is central to my stability and strength.

## DEVELOPING SPIRITUALITY
# Slow Down

We go so fast in our lives. Our days and hours are filled with things we want to do or have to do or think we have to do. A client once said to me, "I'm living my life off of a list."

How easily we have slipped into this fast pace, this high level of activity. We are in fact living in a world that is full of data and opportunities. It is also a world that has many of us filling many roles at once: parent, breadwinner, caretaker of aging parents, housekeeper, mechanic, gardener, homemaker, "chief cook and bottle-washer." We can barely get done in a day what we think needs to be done. And often we don't.

As we speed up and move mindlessly from one activity to the next, bringing our spirituality along with us does not even occur to us. Our mind is busy thinking of what we are going to do next. I know I am guilty of this. I finally caught my self red-handed on this after many years of the same behavior. I noticed that after working hard to put a good meal on my table and after all of the family gathered together to eat it, one of the first phrases out of my mouth once everyone had food on their plate was "After this let's . . ."

"After this let's . . ." What a great way not to slow down and enjoy the fruits of my efforts and the gifts of the present: good food, family time together, silence, relaxation, and who knows what else.

"After this let's . . ." What a great way to keep moving on and not stop. And without a doubt, that was what I was doing. I was feeling the need to keep moving. There were things to do, plans to be made.

But I am realizing those things will happen anyway. So why not slow down for the moment and be there?

Several days each week I start my work-away-from-home day later in the morning. On those mornings, I walk our daughter to her school out here in the country. And then I go on my own walk. I walk for exercise and for meditation. I consider my self so lucky to be able to walk at this time of day. It is so fresh and delightful. Somewhere during the walk each day I stop completely and stand very still.

Standing there, I become increasingly aware of this earth upon which I am standing. I notice the sounds of the birds and the breeze and the river. I see the Blue Ridge Mountains in front of me, and notice the rocks and colors there. I am aware of the steadiness and peacefulness of it all. And I am struck by the fact that all of this will remain as the haven that it is while I run out into the world doing my thing. The creek beside our house will keep flowing over the rocks with its refreshing sounds, and the sun will track its familiar course, warming our home and creating gorgeous lighting as the day nears its end.

Standing still helps me to see all of this and to feel the serenity and stability that come for me by having all of this brought into my awareness. Without my efforts to slow down and even stop, there is a good chance that all of this wonder will pass me by.

DEVELOPING SPIRITUALITY
# Simplify

I can hardly write this morning because of the list in my mind. I went on my morning walk, and my mind chatted on about the things I could do in the one hour I will have this morning before my daughter and I head off to church. It is an unreasonable list that is intrusive and persistent, and each of the items on it beckons me to pick it.

The list goes something like this: Write on your book, finish sewing two pillows for the chairs on our front porch (an incomplete project we worked on yesterday), call my brother and invite him to supper, call my friend about our canoeing plans this afternoon, take a shower, get breakfast for us, get dressed, and go.

I chuckle as I write out this list here. I know it is ridiculous, and seeing it on paper and telling you about it moves it to absurd.

So what I have to do is simplify. For me, I have to do this over and over in a day. Obviously I cannot get all of this done in the period of time I have to do it. In fact, I probably cannot get it done by the end of today. It's just too much.

So I listen to my self and allow things to happen as they will and choose from the list. I have chosen writing over sewing. In my sicker days I would have tried to do both. This morning I am well enough to know better than that.

Simplifying is about weeding out some of the extras so that what we choose to keep can grow and flourish and not be choked out by rushing, anxiety, and frustration.

Simplifying is about editing our lists so that what we choose to keep will be clear and strong, and we will feel clear and strong.

And when we are not choked out by rushing, anxiety, and frustration and when we feel clear and strong, we can better access our spirituality. We can take a breath, be with our self and what we are doing, and make contact with our higher power.

So as I was walking along this morning, practicing letting my thoughts go (and as I have said, it was a good workout for that), I was all of a sudden walking five yards away from two rabbits that were stopped in their tracks. I stopped too. And the three of us stood watching each other for ever so long. I took time to notice their coats and eyes and tails. They did not seem afraid, though they stood still as statues. We were all just standing still on this earth, letting go of our lists for the day and being with each other and our self. A squirrel then crossed the road to join us, but only briefly, as its activity sent the rabbits running off in two directions, the squirrel up a tree, and me on down the road.

But we all stopped and met each other this morning. We simplified life even if it was just for those passing moments. It was delightful and refreshing and a good reminder of what I speak about.

I need to simplify in many aspects of my life, from lists to possessions to thoughts. We clutter our lives with stuff and mental chatter. In so doing, we miss the great moments that are right before our eyes and hearts.

DEVELOPING SPIRITUALITY
# Be in the Present

I was a cheerleader in my high school days. Today as I
was anticipating writing this essay on being in the present,
I remembered a cheer we used to rally the crowds:

> Lean to the left.
>
> Lean to the right.
>
> Stand up.
>
> Sit down.
>
> Fight! Fight! Fight!

Now why would this cheer come to my mind in this context?
My guess is that it reminds me of the way some of my days go:

> Rally here.
>
> Rally there.
>
> Run around
>
> and Do! Do! Do!

This is a chant that stirs me and moves me away from the
moment and into thoughts and action. An adapted version I
have concocted could be said this way:

> Look to the past.
>
> Look ahead.
>
> Worry.
>
> Fret.
>
> We're as good as dead.

Dead? Yes, dead. If I'm into my thoughts, plans, actions, schedules, it's likely that I'm missing the moment that I am in, and so it is as though I were not there.

How many times have we not known if we turned off a burner or turned down the wood stove? We weren't there. How many times do we not remember something someone said to us? We weren't there.

Over and over in the course of a day we leave the present moment. In fact, for me, I have to make a conscious effort to be in the present, reminding my self to hear, see, feel, smell, and experience what is happening right now.

And in bringing my self to the present moment, I discover such richness there, richness in senses and emotions.

And I believe that richness is both spirituality and a tap to deeper spirituality.

Bringing my self to the present moment greatly increases the chances that I can access my spirituality.

When I am in my head and in action I can easily forget the bigger picture. I can forget that there is anyone other than me to see that all of this gets done. I can forget that there is a wonderful world right here and now and a power greater than me at work in it.

Being in the present moment brings me back to life and spirit.

DEVELOPING SPIRITUALITY
# Find Some Solitude

I have been away from this writing for a while. I have let life have me off doing other things. And the whole while I have known that this was the next subject for me to write on: finding solitude.

I have had some resistance in me to putting on paper what I mean here.

Perhaps that is because I have some resistance in my self to finding solitude. I stay busy and move from one thing to another, often with no break in between activities. There is some part of me that just hates to stop what I'm doing until I am finished. And I am never finished.

And being a mother, a wife, a daughter, a sister, a friend, a breadwinner, there is literally no time for solitude from others unless I make sure it happens for me.

Solitude is about time for my self to be with my self. Solitude is about minimizing external distractions and interruptions for a while.

We think of solitude as being especially fostered by being out in nature on a quiet walk in the woods or along a shore. Or we imagine a retreat in a remote area or a sanctuary or meditation space. Yes, each of these places can be a wonderful source of solitude.

Practically speaking, however, these types of places for solitude are not necessarily available to us on a daily, easy-to-access basis. But that is no reason not to find solitude in ways that *can* work for us.

I know that I have a space for my self in my bedroom where I have my books, some possessions from my childhood, tapes, and a comfortable place to sit and/or lie. I also have a couple of places on our property that are good for solitude.

I imagine you are aware of such spaces in your own world, or if not, I suggest that they are there waiting to be found by you.

Sometimes solitude comes simply by closing a door, not answering the phone, and turning off the television, radio, and computer.

Solitude can be had by setting boundaries with others and by prioritizing our self. Getting to this solitude rarely just happens. We have to make it happen for our self. It is a self-imposed time-out.

We have to tell our children, our partner, our parents, our siblings, our friends, our co-workers and clients that we will "get back with them," but we first need to take a break. We need to tell our self that this is okay to do, that it is okay to temporarily let go of our roles and responsibilities in order to restore our self and our spirit.

And we don't have to take a super-long time in solitude to get some benefits. Granted, a day would be great. But certainly let's not wait around for that to happen.

A departure into thirty minutes of solitude can really make a good difference for me when I need to re-center my self. An hour is fabulous. You can learn what is helpful for you. The important point here is that some time in solitude is better than none.

Let's not wait around for the right place and the right time for solitude. It just isn't going to happen. And without it, we get sicker and madder and more anxious and stressed.

Solitude helps us to get back in touch with our physical and emotional self. We can become quieter, calmer, more centered. Our awareness increases and our mind can clear. And we can open our self more to the broader picture of life and the presence of powers greater than our self in and with us.

DEVELOPING SPIRITUALITY

# Breathe

Bring your focus to your breath.

This is in no way a unique idea. Following the breath is a cornerstone of meditation and mindfulness. Wonderful and extensive books have been written on this topic and provide excellent guidelines on using the breath. *The Miracle of Mindfulness* (Nhat Hanh, 1976) and *Wherever You Go, There You Are* (Kabat-Zinn, 1994) are two good examples.

For the purposes of this book, I am simply addressing the importance of bringing our focus back to our breath as a means of calming our self and returning to our self. For some this is a reminder. For others this may be a relatively new notion.

As we get unhealthily attached and entangled, we get further and further away from our self. Such attachments can simply be over trying to get everything on our "To Do" list done for the day or trying to get our children or partners to do something we think they should do.

With entanglements our focus gets more and more on things outside of our self, and at our worst, we are essentially disconnected from our body, mind, heart, and spirit.

Bringing our focus to our breath brings us back to our self. Rather than doing one thing and thinking about another, we are bringing our physical and mental selves into accord. Rather than being riveted on the external, we regain contact with the internal.

Focusing on your breath is a simple and powerful way to almost immediately reconnect with you, which is the heart of the path out of entanglements.

Focusing on your breath means just that: bringing your awareness to your inhalations and exhalations.

* As you inhale, notice the feeling of the air through your nose.

* Notice your chest rise.

* Notice the moment when you slightly pause between the inhalation and exhalation.

* As you exhale, notice your chest fall.

* Notice muscles in your body letting go.

* Repeat this slowly for a while. As you do so, you may find that your breaths are deepening, that you inhale longer and have longer sustained exhales.

* As thoughts come to your mind, simply bring your focus back to your breath over and over.

We can focus on our breath anywhere, anytime. Certainly it is a wonderful way to reconnect with our self when we have some solitude. But again, let's not wait for those special times for renewal.

We can renew our self even in the middle of an argument or a worry if we bring our focus to our breath. When we start feeling driven, anxious, overloaded, and agitated, focusing on our breath can help us to recenter and relax.

I think of following and deepening my breath as a way to reset my internal thermostat. As my breathing deepens, I feel my blood pressure go down, my muscles relax, and my body temperature drop. I am no longer as attached to all of those things that I felt were so important. I am back in touch with my self. I feel calmer, safer, and better able to access my spirituality.

DEVELOPING SPIRITUALITY
# Relax Your Body

The amount of tension we carry around in our body is actually quite remarkable. We put it in our neck, shoulders, and back. We grind our teeth, tighten our jaw. We clench our fists, knot our stomach. We keep a perpetual smile or frown. Our muscles are tight and held.

Sometimes we are aware of this tension. Often we are not.

Entanglements invite us to neglect our physical self. We lose sleep, skip meals, or overeat for comfort. We overextend our bodies to accommodate others and put off routine care, including medical and dental appointments, for our self.

Often we are so out of touch with our self that we are not aware of this tightness and holding in our body until it starts to scream at us in the form of chronic pain or illness.

Making contact with our physical self is very important to disentangling. In fact, contact with our physical self can be an essential door to pass through in order to access other parts of our self, including emotional feelings and spirit.

In his book *Full Catastrophe Living,* Jon Kabat-Zinn uses the body scan as a means of tuning in to the body. With a quiet mind, lie or sit in a comfortable posture and progressively move your focus through your entire body from head to toe or vice versa, noticing any sensations you may have in each body part. For example:

* Starting with your feet, bring your focus to that part of your body.

* Notice any sensations you may have in your feet.

* Notice them making contact with whatever surface on which they may be.

* Notice the feeling of your shoes or socks or the air touching them.

* Really pay attention to your feet: What do you notice?

* And now notice your calves. . . .

Once we are in touch with our body, we can then respond to what it needs. Relaxation is probably one of those needs. Many people I treat in counseling describe their problems as related to being too stressed. And my experience is that when I am entangled with someone else, my stress level is almost chronically present and high.

So relax.

Well, how?

Well, lots of people have lots of ideas that work for them:

* hot showers
* hot tubs
* long walks
* yoga
* reading
* meditation
* deep breathing
* massage
* time with pets
* time with friends
* time alone

* listening to music

* making music

* writing

* mindless television

Get to know your body, paying particular attention to places where you put your tension. Most of us have at least a couple of places we routinely tighten and hold. Find yours. And then respond by letting go and relaxing. Become aware of what helps you to relax your body. And try to do it often.

Relaxing the body brings us back to our self. It calms us, re-centers us, and opens the path to our heart and spirit.

DEVELOPING SPIRITUALITY

# Quiet Your Mind

Entanglements are not about quiet minds. When we are entangled with someone else, our mind just chats on and on about him or her. It doesn't matter whether we are with that person or not. We think about what he or she is doing. We think about what we said, what we wish we had said, or what we wish we hadn't said to him or her. We think about how he or she may feel about us, what he or she said or may say to us. And on and on.

We are preoccupied.

And our mind gets worn out.

And we are bound to lose our self.

If our mind is so busy with all of these thoughts about the past and future and about things outside of our self, then we are not paying any attention to our self.

Quieting our mind is important to disentangling. We need to become aware of the busyness of our thinking and learn to manage it. We need to notice these obsessive thoughts and intervene on our own behalf. We cannot begin to disentangle until we learn to quiet this thinking of ours.

Many of us find this hard to do. Some believe it is almost impossible to do. I believe it can be done with conscious effort on our part and practice. Quieting the mind involves having the ability to dismiss thoughts. It means we can consciously choose whether to think about something or not. We can say to our self, "I'll think about that later," or "I'm going to stop thinking about that because I can't do anything about that now."

We can quiet our mind by repeatedly bringing our self back into the present.

Bringing our focus to our breath can instantly bring us out of our head and into the moment.

Reminders to our self that we are worrying about things way too far ahead or too far in the past can help to bring us here now.

Reminders to our self that we are thinking about things over which we have no control can be useful in letting go and resting our mind.

To quiet the mind, we need first to get in touch with its chatter. That should not be hard to do.

Then we need to make a decision to let go of these thoughts. We need to have had enough of them and to have the desire to be free of them.

And then we need to find a way of quieting the mind that works for us. Many of the ideas already described in this section on spirituality can help with this:

* Slow down.
* Simplify.
* Be in the present.
* Find some solitude.
* Breathe.
* Relax your body.

We need to be kind to our self as we work on quieting our mind. It is normal for our heads to be full of thoughts, so don't criticize your self for the way your thoughts jump back in there. And don't give up on learning how to quiet them. You can do it with practice.

And the benefits are tremendous. You can take a break from those old mental tapes you have played and played in your head. You can clear your head. You can have an empty, resting mind. And by so doing you may well have some peace and find that you want to make some changes in those old mental tapes.

## DEVELOPING SPIRITUALITY
# Sit in Silence

On a daily basis our minds are full of thoughts, and we have lists of lists. We rush from one activity to another, and while we are busy with one activity we are thinking about the next one: "When we finish this, let's . . ."

And when we are entangled, our minds and days can be even fuller and busier. Not only do we have our own lists in our minds, but also we may have lists for others—lists of what they should do, lists of what they haven't done, lists of what we wish they would do. We have imaginary thoughts of others that go on and on. Some are fun; some disturb us.

All of this fills our mind and our time.

The notion of stopping all of this for a while and sitting in silence is a healthy one, but some of us do not naturally move toward it. We get so caught up in these thoughts and lists and rush without awareness from one to another. We are reluctant to stop for even a brief while to be quiet. We are so afraid that we won't get done what we believe needs to be done that we "just can't stop."

And some of us just don't like to be in a stopped, silent place. It is too uncomfortable, unfamiliar, scary.

But rather than being "a waste of time" or "another thing on our list," sitting in silence can be a refueling of our self. Sitting in silence can help us stop this thinking and doing *ad nauseam* and help us to see things more clearly and with improved perspective. It can help us to reconnect us with our self.

A dear friend of mine suggested that we pause in between each of our daily activities for several minutes and do nothing.

To that idea I add the suggestion that in those breaks we turn off the television or stereo; that we put aside our newspapers and other reading materials; that we decline conversations in the room, on the phone, or on the computer. This is not a time to do that "little extra something."

This is a time to do nothing and to be silent.

There are numerous opportunities for this in our day as we become aware of them. One of those moments I have noticed I call a "Microwave Moment."

One evening at work I popped my meal into the microwave for four minutes. I *immediately* thought, "Now, what can I do for four minutes? A phone call? Some copying?" And then I caught my self red-handed in this using-every-minute mode, in this nonstop rushing from one thing to another. And I told my self, "No. Just sit still. How about doing nothing for four minutes? How about just being silent and present in this quiet moment?" And so I had my Microwave Moment.

Silence can be restful. Silence can be our friend. Silence can be scary, too, if we are afraid of what may come up for us without our busyness to defend our self.

But defending our self through busyness is not really protecting our self as much as losing our self. Our busyness takes us away from our thoughts, feelings, and general awareness. It invites us to lose our self in whatever else we are doing or thinking. It invites us to lose our self in other people and other things.

A break into silence is a direct invitation to come back to our self, to listen to nothing other than our breathing and to notice, only notice, what physical and emotional sensations are present in and with us.

I am sure there are daily opportunities for you to indulge in this silence, if only for moments. I invite you to become aware of them and practice sitting with them for your self.

DEVELOPING SPIRITUALITY
# Discover Your Higher Power

Surely all we have to do to accept the idea of a power greater than our self is to look at the world around us.

Just this morning my husband, daughter, and I walked a trail in a Vermont state park. Gorgeous ferns proliferated on the ground and on rocks. Numerous brooks ran off the side of the hill, creating pools surrounded by moss-covered rocks. Silver maples and birch reached high into the sky. The loons cried out from the lake below. The balance and cycles of the natural world surrounded and filled us.

A power greater than my self was at work here.

We look at our children, at flowers, at vegetables, at animal life and know there is a power greater than our self.

In less immediately tangible ways, we can also come to know there is a power greater than our self. Our higher power can offer us wisdom, strength, guidance, comfort, and protection beyond what we can do or imagine.

Those of us prone to entanglements sometimes act as if we are fully in charge and fully responsible for everything. The notion of a power greater than our self does not come to our mind (because it is so cluttered) nor to our spirit (because we are so out of touch with it).

Very important to disentangling is discovering your higher power. It is important for us to save our self by not relying completely on our own personal resources. We can and do exhaust them, and those resources alone cannot get us out of our entanglements and to the happiness we seek anyway.

You see, entanglements involve our deeply believing that we know what is best for us and others, and we pursue those ends with a vengeance and, again, with a belief that we know how to achieve those ends.

This is where we get into deep trouble with our self, where we cannot see or allow that perhaps we may not know what is best for us or others and that there is a power greater than our self that is with us and supporting us. There is a higher power to whom or to which we can let things go that are beyond our control.

Discovering your higher power is up to you. This is a personal decision and relationship. Those of you who have a God you know and rely on through your religious beliefs probably have this God as your higher power. Those of you who do not subscribe to a particular religious faith may discover your higher power in any form you wish: man, woman, spirit, animal, within you, within a group, in nature—to name just a few.

Discovering your higher power means you decide that you are not the whole show and that there is also a power that is at work with a bigger picture, more resources, and greater wisdom.

Our task is to slow our self down, quiet our pushing and pulling, and set out to hear, feel, and experience the constant presence of our higher power.

DEVELOPING SPIRITUALITY

# Have an Ongoing Relationship with Your Higher Power

The important part of this idea about your higher power is that your relationship be ongoing. The twelve-step programs describe this as conscious contact with our higher power, which helps us bring our spirituality into all areas of our life.

Awakening to the higher power in our lives is not just about calling upon that power once a day, occasionally, or when trouble appears.

The idea here of a spirituality that heals us involves a constant, ongoing relationship with our higher power. Our contact with that power can be made moment by moment in ways that are personal and comfortable: prayer, meditation, conversations, walks, silence, and breathing, to mention only a few.

I think of this as developing a relationship with my higher power. In order to have a relationship, I need to spend time with my higher power, listening to that power and trusting it. I can do these things in a silent wood, in the middle of a meeting, or during an argument at home. I often make sure I'm in touch with my higher power as I enter what I anticipate will be a difficult situation. I am in touch with my higher power when I feel good and grateful.

You see, entanglements are essentially the opposite of spirituality and contact with our higher power. Entanglements strip us of our spirit. Without knowing it, we are selling our soul—and all the rest of our self, too—to someone else in the hope that this will create the relationship we are seeking. It is not even that he or she is asking this of us. We just decide, consciously or not, that such giving of our self will produce the end that we desire.

But it does not. Instead we find our self tense, anxious, and frequently trying to manipulate and control people and situations, even in ways that may seem useful and kind. And we feel empty.

We need not give our souls to anyone. Disentangling is about seeing how we do this and working on stopping it. Cultivating an ongoing relationship with our higher power is an important aspect of ending this soul giveaway.

Cultivating a relationship with our higher power will strengthen our ability to cultivate a healthy relationship with someone else.

When we have a healthy, ongoing relationship with our higher power, we can learn when to let go of things beyond our control, and we have the backup support of our higher power to be with us as we do let go of these things to which we have clung so tightly.

When we have a healthy, ongoing relationship with our higher power, we can have comfort when we are afraid, company when we are confused, and support when we need to act. We don't have to seek these things so adamantly and exclusively from others. They are in and with us all the time.

Yes, you will lose contact with your higher power throughout a day. I certainly do. All of a sudden I catch my self trying to force some solution, trying to make something happen, being too attached to doing or getting something, and I back off by reconnecting with my higher power. I do this over and over through the course of a day: entangle/let go.

So don't be discouraged when you find your self out there again, ripping and tearing, trying to make everything happen on your own.

With an ongoing relationship with our higher power, all we have to do is become aware of when we have lost contact and are trying to control things over which we have no control, and then simply reconnect. The relief that follows can be great

DEVELOPING SPIRITUALITY
# Let Go of Things You Cannot Control

Several years ago I was explaining disentangling to an interested person to whom this was a relatively novel idea. One of the things I said was that disentangling involves "letting go."

"Letting go of what?" she asked.

I paused briefly to think, not wanting disentangling to come across as passive or as giving up or giving in.

"Disentangling is about learning to let go of things we have no control over," I responded.

"Oh," she said with a hint of informed reflection.

Many of our entanglements come from trying to control things over which we have no control. And often we don't have a clue we're doing this. We think that what we are doing for or to the other person is kind, helpful, important, logical, natural, desirable. We get so caught up in our own notions about how we think things are or how we want things to be that we are not in touch with whether we can or cannot do something about them.

We act as though we can do something about everything.

But we can't.

And knowing the difference between what we can and cannot control is essential to disentangling. Figuring out what we can and cannot control can be a challenge sometimes. Without our awareness we jump right in there to make something happen or to fix something, and we are entangled again.

Here are some general notions about what we can and cannot control:

We can control:

* where we are.

* whom we are with.

* what we think.

* what we do with our money, time, possessions.

* how we handle our feelings.

We cannot control:

* where other people go.

* whom they are with.

* what they think.

* what they do with their money, time, possessions.

* how they handle their feelings.

Now, an important point of clarification here: We are trying to learn to identify what we cannot control and then to let go of trying to control it. This is so we don't keep beating our head against a wall and burning up our good time, energy, and spirit.

This does not mean, however, that you have to put up with unacceptable behaviors from someone else.

You may identify some things that you cannot control and simply let them go. For example,

You have been wanting a friend to apply for a job you believe is perfect for him, but he hasn't made even one call about it. You have talked to your friend at least three times about this with no real response of interest.

It's probably time to let go.

You may identify some other things that you cannot control *and* that you cannot live with. For example,

> Your partner is frequently critical of you. He insults your efforts and discourages you in the things you enjoy. He will call you derogatory names and make fun of you in front of others. You have repeatedly told him to stop all this behavior, but he hasn't stopped.

> You can't make him stop, but you don't have to live with it, either. This is where boundaries come in. You can tell your self and him that you won't do _____ if he continues to do these things.

Whether we are letting go of things beyond our control that we can or cannot live with, the process of letting go can be helped by our spirituality.

Spirituality reminds us of the bigger picture, which we often cannot see for the picture we are creating in our mind.

Spirituality provides the arena into which we let things go that we cannot control, an arena into which we can relinquish responsibility with trust and faith—not faith that things will happen as we want them to, but faith that life will unfold as it will and that we will be okay.

DEVELOPING SPIRITUALITY
# Practice These Things

Earlier in this book I wrote about the basic features of disentangling. One of those features is that disentangling is a process that takes time. It takes a while for us to make the emotional, behavioral, and spiritual changes I am talking about here. One important action on your part to help with these changes is to practice these ideas.

By practice, I mean at least two things.

Practice here means to try some or all of these ideas in the spirit of learning how to do them and of improving your performance of them. This is like practicing our piano lessons or basketball shots. Only by bringing our self to the situation with awareness and focus and then taking risks to learn how to do something new will we be able to disentangle with skill and serenity.

Practice here also means to bring your practice of these ideas for disentangling into your daily life. Make them part of your way of life. Don't save them for emergencies, grabbing them like ammunition from a stockade. Inasmuch as weapons can be dangerous if we are not skilled and practiced in their use, the ideas for disentangling can blow up in our face or backfire on us if we haven't worked to incorporate them into our lives with deep understanding and with a healthier self.

Daily practice of our spirituality is especially important. Practicing our spirituality can calm us, recenter us, and clear our brains. Spirituality can provide our anchor in the storms we encounter. But again, in order to know where that anchor is and how to use it effectively, we need to have brought it into our daily practice.

Now, I say daily but I don't really mean just once a day. My experience is that I am in contact with my spirituality/higher power many times in the course of the day. When things are good, when things are bad, when there's nothing much happening at all—all of these are opportunities for me to practice my spirituality.

So how do you practice? What does this act mean? Well, again, that's going to be personal to you. In this section on cultivating spirituality I've suggested many ideas to help you access your spirituality: slow down, relax the body, quiet the mind, breathe, etc. In the same way that each of us gets to know our own higher power, we can each develop our own practice that helps us to access that power and reap the benefits of our relationship with it.

So figure out what your practice of your spirituality looks like. Maybe you already know and follow your practice. Keep it up. And maybe this is new to you, in which case try different avenues for contact with your self and your higher power and see what feels good to you. And then practice that contact.

Practice means that we are weaving spirituality into our lives. Inasmuch as threads woven together can create a beautiful fabric, the daily practice of spirituality in our lives can help to create a lovely and strong self.

DEVELOPING SPIRITUALITY

# Cultivate Faith

I have some memories of my journey to cultivate faith. When I started my work on disentangling, I remember feeling lonely. I was doing the things I understood would help me to get the emotional distance I needed, but in the process I was feeling disconnected and alone. I felt skeptical about what I was doing and fearful that this was all I was going to get out of the process: empty distance.

I remember talking to some friends about this, friends who were ahead of me on this path. They understood what I was talking about. They had been there, too. And they said that as they continued to grow and develop a healthy separateness from others, they felt less and less lonely.

I told my self that if I had faith, I, too, would eventually feel more comfortable with my separateness and not experience it as loneliness. I told my self to just keep practicing my new ways and have faith that they would help me to feel more serene and content with my self, by my self.

At a later time on my journey, I was speaking with one of my mentors about making a big change in my life. I remember seeing this potential change as a great risk. I did not know what would happen if I made that change. I had no idea how others would react to it or what they might do. I had no idea what I would do or how I would feel if I made this change in my life. All of these unknowns frightened me greatly and for years had kept me from taking some action.

My mentor's response to all of this was to warmly and gently remind me that to make these changes required "a leap of faith" on my part.

The controlling, exacting part of me wants to know precisely what will happen when changes occur: If _____, then _____. But no, life does not work this way. Often we have to make a decision or a change that we have calculated to be in our best interest without having any idea what the fallout will be.

This is where faith is everything.

Faith creates a bridge for us from the known to the unknown, from who we are today to who we may become. Faith enables us to move on things that have had us stuck. Faith enables us to do things we didn't think we could do, to continue when we didn't think we could.

And what is this faith in? As with the other areas of spirituality and higher power, faith is to be designed by you. For me, faith is that there is a bigger picture out there, bigger than the one I'm seeing and managing, and I believe I need to do my part *and* allow that bigger picture to unfold as well. It is a blend of taking responsibility within my limits and allowing life to simultaneously unfold, being present and aware and responding as is healthy for me.

My faith is my trust in this process of living this way. My faith is in my ongoing relationship with my higher power that helps me to believe that I am okay and that what I need will be or actually is here already.

Faith comes with time. It is a deeper aspect of spirituality that we can come to know as we travel on our path, making scary changes and feeling alone. Faith is the light in our dark times and an ever-present source of comfort and strength. I rarely feel lonely anymore.

DEVELOPING SPIRITUALITY
# Spirituality and You

**Take a moment to consider
spirituality in your present life:**

Is spirituality present?

Is it important to you?

Does it make a difference in your life?

Do you see any value in it?

Would you like to make any
changes in your spirituality?


**If you find your self wanting to make spirituality
more a part of your life, then read on.
Consider what you already do in your
life that cultivates your spirituality and
jot down some of those ideas.**

How do you make contact with your spirituality?

How often do you access your spirituality,
and under what circumstances?

**Now review the list of ideas in this past
section on spirituality. Maybe you can simply
look at the list in the table of contents to
give your self an overview of the ideas.**

Which of the ideas naturally appeal
to you most at this time?

Which of the ideas interest you as something
you would like to add to your life?

Which of the ideas can be realistically
added to your current life situation?

**Considering all of these ideas, what are
present paths you wish to develop in
order to cultivate your spirituality?**

What do you want to keep doing?

What do you want to add as ways
to develop your spirituality?

What are obstacles to your doing these things?

What can you do to resolve these obstacles?

**Imagine what your life might be
like with greater spirituality.**

I never realized this *thirst* for new things.

Life is too short to be hurt by others.

I'm starting to think: "What do *I* want?"

Breath of fresh air is in my head.

# living

(as celebrated by various people along the way)

"Disentangling helps me to feel free and loving at the same time."

*Rebecca, age 20*

# 8

# So What's Happened to "Others on This Journey"?

It's been two years since I started writing this book. It's been quite fun and inspiring to do so. I've enjoyed taking the time to think through the specifics of disentangling and to write down many of the wonderful things that have been said by my clients and me over the last six years as we've worked together on this topic.

As I neared the end of the writing in Chapter Seven on all the ideas of disentangling, I started to anticipate the writing of this chapter, which is a follow-up to the fictionalized characters in Chapter Four who are based on my real clients. The core of this book has always been the detailed ideas of disentangling as presented in Chapter Seven. It has only been as I have written this book that I have realized that I want to also include parts of my story and the stories of others.

Now that I have done so, it makes so much sense in terms of helping each of you to see in a practical way the issues with which we get entangled, the ways we get entangled, the ways we act when we are all caught up in something, and the ways we have of getting stuck there if we are not wise and careful.

As I started thinking about this chapter, my thoughts were to simply tell you in general terms what has happened to each of the characters I introduced in Chapter Four. Most of the clients on whom they are based are no longer in therapy, but I have been in contact with many of them in direct and indirect ways over the years. Thus, I knew I had enough data to say something to you about each of them that would be true and useful.

It then dawned on me to interview each of the clients personally to gather specific feedback about their use or nonuse of disentangling ideas and the changes they have experienced in their lives as a result of their use or nonuse of them. Here I've written a whole book about this process, believing that it is very useful; however, it became clear to me that there are more people out there than just me who are trying these ideas and who can speak to their effectiveness.

So I went seeking their words and their stories, their experiences and their current relationship issues.

I found all seven clients and they were more than willing to talk with me. Most were quite enthusiastic about this book and eager to provide more input. I sent them each a copy of the fictionalized character I based on them. Additionally, I wrote a two-page questionnaire that I sent to them explaining that I would use it to structure our follow-up interview. As we met for the interview, I took extensive notes on what they said, quoting them as often as possible and checking back with them to make sure I had heard them correctly.

How wonderful it was to talk with each of them. How exciting it was to speak this common language of disentangling with each other and to understand their issues and their successes. My clients have always been an important part of the development of these disentangling ideas, and I felt their involvement more strongly than ever as we met.

After these meetings, I studied my notes on the structured interview forms and then wrote the results from the interviews with the fictionalized character in mind. The fictionalization is of the details of the characters, their lives, and the people in their stories, and the fictionalization follows up directly with the characters in Chapter Four. What is real are the words said by my clients about their application of disentangling ideas and the effects of those efforts.

So now that you've read through the disentangling ideas and have more of an understanding of what this process is about, join me as we hear the voices of others out there who are applying these ideas in their daily lives.

# Elizabeth

Elizabeth and I are sitting in a Chinese restaurant having lunch and talking about what has been going on in her life over the last couple of years, during which time she has no longer been in psychotherapy. She is once again her reliable, prepared self. Prior to our interview today, she completed the questionnaire that I sent her in advance. We are not rushed today and know that we can talk privately in our booth for as long as we wish.

It is with Elizabeth that the original list for disentangling began. When we last heard from Elizabeth in Chapter Four, she was struggling to figure out how to deal with her deteriorating relationship with her husband. She found her self easily and quickly trapped in "help me/don't help me" arguments initiated by her husband. As we began talking about listening and detachment in 1992, she had said to me, "Detachment is very hard for me. . . . How would you do that?"

Today Elizabeth says that her life is "fundamentally better than ever." Roughly two years ago, she left her home and then her marriage. She had hung on and worked on her self and her relationship with her husband as long as she could. She worked in individual therapy, and they tried marital counseling for a while also. But "nothing helped. . . . I am convinced that he wanted to end it without saying so. Thus, no guilt to him.

"I miss living in a partnership in many ways, but I'm realizing or remembering how little I really had of a partnership."

What finally sent Elizabeth out the door of their home were the ways her husband's treatment of her were interfering with her relationship with their only child. Elizabeth says, "He had gone right over the edge," referring to his actions and statements that commonly excluded her from activities he and their daughter were doing.

"Talking about facing illusions, it was clear to me that he didn't want me back when he sent me my groceries." She elaborates, "And I'm still facing illusions about my marriage. Recent realization: There were never enough horses for all three of us to ride together; now that I am gone there are plenty of horses for all."

Elizabeth reflects on the original reasons that brought her to therapy. She states with conviction, "I needed to be able to have my head for my own use."

She asks, "Did I tell you my story about the green pot holders?"

"I don't believe so," I say.

"Well, as I was setting up housekeeping in my new home, I needed to buy some pot holders. So I went to the store, and as I was standing there looking at the display of pot holders, I thought, 'If I had a favorite color, what would it be?' I was so struck to realize that I had no idea what *I* liked. For decades I have deferred to the color preferences of others living in our home, and so I've always lived with blue. I was quite surprised to realize this. I bought green pot holders."

And this is said by a woman with a doctorate degree and a job in a high level of management, a woman capable of making important and competent decisions. But in her personal life, her self was absent, unknown, voiceless.

In talking about what has helped Elizabeth to end her marriage and move on in her life feeling "pretty good," she states, "Boundaries. Boundaries. Boundaries. . . . I'm not letting anyone tell me what I think or feel, or spray anger about my home. I'm glad to talk about anything when sentences start with 'I' and the tone is mutually respectful."

She says that she uses self-talk to give her self permission to detach and set boundaries and to help her stick with her limits: "This is not my problem." "I need to go now." "I'm okay with my self about this."

Elizabeth says, "I make one short statement. I say things once and then stop. If I think I am about to get caught up in an old 'game,' I just walk away."

Spirituality is central for Elizabeth. "It's the center. With entangling we're not in the center."

It is good to remember that when we first met Elizabeth, she was a good problem-solver and "fixer." She still is; however, she says that she now knows her limits in fixing self and others. And she says, "It has been very healthy and healing for me to pray for my ex-husband's peace and happiness, replacing my old prayer for God to 'fix' my marriage and fix me. P.S.: I'm not broken."

"So what are things you do to foster your spirituality?" I ask.

"Quietly sitting, prayer, church choir, reading the Bible, feminist literature, archeology. . . . It's interesting," she says, "how these things we do to center our self are the opposite of what we were taught to do and what would not get us approval early on.

"Now," she says, "I want more time for this part of my life, so I'm setting boundaries on other parts and others' wants."

Meanwhile, she says that her present relationship with her now ex-husband is "better than anytime in the last decade." And about her relationship with her daughter, Elizabeth says, "We are really making progress . . . so healthy!"

## Anne

Anne has been working on her self for years. She worked in weekly individual therapy and was an active and longtime member of our Disentangle Group in my private practice. At this time, Anne comes once a month for an individual therapy session to process whatever is going on in her life. She says that rather than take medication for the low-grade and often-present depression she experiences, she strongly prefers to maintain her therapy work. It *is* her medication.

Today, Anne has stayed for a second hour's session after her therapy appointment for us to do our follow-up interview for this book. Anne, too, has prepared in advance by writing out answers to my questionnaire. She is eager to talk.

Anne says that her life is "certainly a lot better than when we started our work years ago. . . . I've used a lot of this [i.e., disentangling ideas]. . . . It has kept my head above water."

She elaborates: "For years, I didn't even enjoy life. Now I believe I am past that and look forward to things. . . . I feel more in control of my life and am happier."

One of Anne's original issues was her belief and fear that all of her problems with work and her marriage were *her* fault: "Is it me? . . . Was I wrong?"

Anne says that she no longer believes that she is the total problem. She has gotten clearer on her identity and feels more confident. This is particularly true in her marriage. "My love life is fine. . . . We are happily married, both working on the relationship."

"So what helped?" I ask.

"A number of things," she says. "Having a therapist that I click with has been very important. And I've learned to stay centered on my self and to take charge of my self. It used to be so easy for me to immediately lose my self in whatever my husband was saying to me about me and what I should be doing."

She continues, "I try not to be driven by trying to please or live up to someone else's illusions or expectations of me.

"And I am not trying to fix, change, or convince my husband to see things my way. . . . I change what I have the power to change and accept what I can't change.

"Then there's detachment," she says. "I've learned when to shut up and not fuel the fires. I won't argue or pursue. I say what I need to say. I do what I need to do. And I set boundaries when I need to set them. I used to not know how to do these things or even that it was okay to do them.

"And I also use self-talk a lot, especially at times of stress or times of not understanding a situation, or when I feel a loss of control.

"Our work together helped me to see my illusions so clearly. This helped me so much. I used to believe, 'I'll have a picture-perfect family. I'll be this wonderful executive and hobnob with all the powers-that-be.' Now I find that when I let go of my illusions, I am less frustrated. Sometimes I don't even realize they are illusions for a long time. But seeing reality and letting go of them sure can be a relief."

"So what about you and work now?" I ask.

"I am still not finding my niche there," she says honestly. "I still have questions about me as a person and what I am doing with my life. I still feel in a limbo state about this. As you know, I have held several jobs over the years very successfully, but I have still never felt really comfortable and confident about what I was doing in my work.

"But I know I'm not all bad. In fact, I'm a good person, a dependable person, who is a hard worker. I'm sure I'm doing what is right for me with work right now. I'm running one of our family's businesses and am very excited about the ideas I have for it.

"I'll just keep taking one day at a time, putting things in the hands of my higher power, setting realistic and easy goals for my self, and avoiding creating illusions, which can increase my stress."

Anne, who is obviously a big fan of disentangling, adds as we are ending, "Disentangling is a great concept and tool for regaining life and self."

# Charlotte

I had not been in contact with Charlotte for several years until I called her for this follow-up interview. Previously, Charlotte was in individual therapy with me and then joined the Disentangle Group for a year or so. She stopped therapy because she was at a point where she was satisfied with her progress and was ready to be out on her own without the regular support of therapy.

When I called Charlotte for this appointment, she was her delightful self, with friendliness and warmth in her voice. She said she would be glad to meet with me and explained that she still works for the travel agency but only half time, so a late morning appointment would be good.

We meet as scheduled in my office the week before Christmas. Charlotte brings her laughter with her and her apologies for not remembering to bring her copy of the questionnaire with her. She has some of her old nervousness and self-consciousness with her, but as we begin to talk, it is clear that she has more strength and a greater foundation.

"So how are you?" I ask.

"I think, good, really. I'm doing things for my self. You know, no one ever told me that it was important or okay to take care of me. I started Nautilus in November, and I'm only working half time so I can have more time with the kids and be at home. I'm pretty comfortable with my life now."

We start to look back at the entanglements with which she was involved when we were working together.

"What has happened to your relationship with your husband?" I ask.

"I'm still married. My relationship still has its ups and downs and can be really frustrating for me. I guess you could say parts of it can still be tangled for me. I slip back."

She continues, "I keep thinking maybe he'll change, but I know he won't. That's the illusion I have to keep working with. . . . It's interesting how now my daughter Christy acts toward him like I used to act. She nags at him about things he does and does not do. I'm trying to help her learn what I've learned, and that is my limit in being able to change someone else and the need to take care of my self."

"And how else do you deal with your 'slips'?" I ask.

"I pray a lot. I have grown in my spirituality through my involvement with my church. When you're closer to God, more things roll off your back and you focus on something else. I have good friends through my church who are wise to my work on setting boundaries and centering my self. They've been known to remind me, 'Don't get your self started' when they can see that I'm about to launch into my upset over my husband or my mother-in-law."

"And how about that relationship with your mother-in-law? That relationship, too, used to cause you a great deal of frustration and doubt."

"Well, I've just learned to set a lot of boundaries with her. If I need to say no, I say no. If I'm not in the mood to deal with her, I don't. She's still always saying things that make us feel guilty. But I've learned I can't change that and that's how she is. I don't have to take the guilt."

"You sound like you know what you're talking about," I comment on hearing this.

"I believe I do," she responds with confidence. "I've had to do this same thing with boundaries and firmness with this co-worker of mine, too. I just use lots of 'I' statements with her and am clear with her and my self that I'm not going to clean up her messes.

"You know, another thing that helps me is to talk with my sister who understands all of this stuff. We get on the phone and talk about the crazies that have shaken our lives. It's good to talk with her, to laugh about the insanity, and to talk about how we are handling things now."

She continues, "When I can feel my self losing control over me, I try to stop and think, not just keep going. I ask my self, 'What's the problem here now? What's happening?' I go into my self and try to become aware of my feelings and needs. This really helps me to regain control over my self."

In a summarizing way, she says, "You know, as I talk, I realize that it's all of the pieces of disentangling working together that help me. It feels good to review it."

And I agree. It feels good to me to be with Charlotte, to review all of this with her, and to see the ways she's bringing comfort and confidence into her life.

"I just don't want to leave," she adds as she lingers when our interview is done.

# Mark

Mark has been gone from therapy for four years. When I went to call him about this possible follow-up interview, I was not sure I would be able to reach him, much less engage him in this process. His hours are long and unpredictable, and I did not know how he would feel about revisiting his issues.

With only two rounds of telephone tag, I was able to reach him, and he expressed a true willingness to come back to talk with me. After studying both of our schedules a good while, we found an evening appointment that would work after we both finished our regularly scheduled day.

Mark entered my office with his usual friendliness and humor. He is witty with some cynicism, and is readily engaged in conversation. He brings pictures of his daughters who are both now teenagers, and he speaks lovingly and comfortably about the good relationship he has with them. He has them half of the time and is glad for this. Spending time with them is a priority for him, and he is clearly enjoying being an active part of their growing up, as shown by the stories he tells me about things they are doing.

"So how are you?" I ask.

"Moderately good," he responds. "My life is dictated by my work, but that is a roller coaster of my own making."

He then starts directly into telling me about a difficult employee situation he has had to deal with recently that required he use some of the ideas for disentangling.

"I had to fire a nurse. She was playing one person against another in our office. She was testing both personal and professional boundaries. It felt very bad and very dangerous.

I felt that I was being used. It made me grateful I had gone through all the stuff I had with my ex-wife. You remember, she used to be my office manager, and she caused me some of these same types of problems."

"So what did you do?" I ask.

"I had to set strong, clear boundaries with her. When she approached me about a possible relationship with her, I said, 'No way.' I finally had to ask her to pack her stuff and to leave our business with no notice."

"And so what about your relationship with your ex-wife, Lynne?"

"I find my self still angry with her for leaving me the way she did. It hurts. I don't think the emotions will ever be gone."

"So how do you deal with that?"

"I try to face the reality of the situation. I remind my self of how much chaos and mistrust she created and how hard it would have been to make things work. It's unfortunate that she was damaged in the ways she was early on. I grieve for the loss of the dreams I had of who she was and possibly could be.

"How the hell would this have worked?" he exclaims as a way to punctuate what he was just explaining.

"And I get to practice these thoughts all of the time. I still live in the house we all lived in. Since she worked in my office, I find her name on old files and papers all the time. And she's still friends with some of the other people who work in the office, so occasionally she calls and fills them in on things in her life. I don't want to hear about it, and I have told my employees that.

"And you know, that reminds me of other boundaries I'm setting for my self at work. It's so easy for me to cross over. So what I do now is listen to my employees' personal problems if they bring them up, but I don't get involved. It's not my job to fix them."

Our discussion about facing illusions continues as I ask Mark whether he has any new, significant relationships in his life now.

"No I don't. My world is kind of limited. It's like another job to me to try to go out. It takes too much energy. And you know, I've realized that in my past relationship, I manipulated both Lynne and my self by trying to be something I am not. I tried to please her, to second-guess her, to satisfy all of her needs without being true to my self. That just took too much work, and I don't want to do that again. So I guess I'm just staying at a distance from relationships until I am ready to start again in this new way."

He continues, "I keep telling my self that 'No one would be interested in you anyway because of all the crazy hours you work and how unavailable you are at times.' Then I realize that *I* don't like my lifestyle. *I* am not happy with the way my life is centered around my work. This is not a way to live forever."

"So I hear ways you are using in facing illusions and boundary setting in your life now. What about spirituality?" I ask.

"It's still hard for me to access spirituality. I am still so tied up with the pervasiveness of religion in my family. This colors it all for me. You remember what a religious fanatic my mother was. I was raised with the belief of total selflessness. I was taught that some bad shit's going to happen anytime, and we need to be ready. Our life was one of great withholding, withholding of attention, affection, and goods. We were told that you don't get anything back until you're damn dead."

His anger and stuckness are so well expressed.

198

He continues, "I do try in my secular way to relieve suffering and to connect with what people are feeling. And I do keep working to free my self from the beliefs and scars left by my mother's religiosity."

By this time we have talked for two hours. Mark comments, "I haven't felt this comfortable and relaxed in a long time. It's good to talk about all of this. I know that I must keep working on getting more time for my self in my life. A lot of things will be helped for me by that."

# Lindsey

Lindsey graduated from college four years ago. She came by to see me occasionally after graduating, but I have not seen her for a couple of years. So when I started to try to get in touch with her about this follow-up interview, I was not sure if I would find her. With a bit of research, however, directory assistance and I were able to find a likely telephone number for her, which I immediately dialed. It was lunchtime, and I fully expected to get an answering machine, hopefully at the correct house.

Much to my surprise, Lindsey answered the phone. We were each quite glad to hear the other's voice. Lindsey explained that I had caught her coming home for lunch. She completed her master's degree in social work last year and is now working in therapeutic foster care. She sets her own schedule, as she works with many of her clients in their homes.

I explained my project to Lindsey, and she quickly showed great enthusiasm. If my memory serves me correctly, the word "disentangle," as used in the context of this book, was first used by Lindsey and me in her therapy sessions. And Lindsey was instrumental in helping to start a Disentangle Group.

Lindsey and I set a telephone appointment time for her interview, remembering to allow for the fact that we would be talking from different time zones. I mailed Lindsey a copy of her description from Chapter Four as well as the questionnaire so that we could fully use our telephone time.

The interview took place the following week. In general, Lindsey says she's "doing pretty well." She elaborates, "I finished my MSW; I am celebrating my second wedding anniversary; and we just bought a house.

"You know I married Thomas?" she asks.

"Well, I figured that out as I was researching your phone number," I respond. Thomas was her hometown boyfriend throughout much of college. She had always told me they would marry even though their relationship was at times on and off and an important topic in her therapy work.

"We are committed to being together. I really want it to work."

We begin to look at her relationships in more detail, and Lindsey makes it clear that she has experienced some important and good changes in her relationships *and* is struggling with other relationship issues. Clearly she is still on her path of self-awareness and growth.

"So what happened to your relationship with your mother?" I ask.

"I have made the most headway with her. Our relationship is 100 percent better. I 'conquered the demon' when I started facing the reality that she is an unhappy, depressed person who I cannot change. I get what I need from her now, and I know not to expect anything more from her."

She continues, "I can't tell you how important it is for me to face my illusions. Of all the ideas for disentangling, this is both the hardest and the most useful for me. I still find my self slipping into illusions easily, especially illusions that seek excitement and attention from males. You know, I don't feel like I really had the love of my mother and father, so I find my self still seeking it from others, especially males. I crave male attention. I want someone to tell me that I'm pretty and smart and attractive.

"I can still be drawn to unhealthy, dysfunctional people. It is a constant struggle for my self to stay with the reality of people and situations and not lose my self to this excitement that still lures me. Reality is more how I want it to be."

"You mention your dad. How are things in your relationship with him now?" I ask.

"I'm having to form a new relationship with him that I'm working on right now. I see him about twice a year, and we talk every week. Like my relationship with my mother, I also always wanted him to be different than he is. He was not a great dad. He was not involved. I've recently realized that he doesn't really listen or even know me. So now I'm working on facing this reality and building a relationship from here with him. I am really trying to apply detachment and boundaries in dealing with him, too."

"And what are you doing to detach and set boundaries?" I ask.

"I notice when I'm all stirred up by talking with him. Then I remind my self that I need to be an adult. I try to be honest with him *and* to ask my self what I can and cannot handle right here and now with him. And you know, I still often use the image of 'one foot in and one foot out' to help me keep my balance and center as I deal with an important relationship. It's so hard!"

"And how about spirituality?"

Lindsey says, "For some reason, spirituality still is my last priority. It constantly nags at me. I wonder what my resistance is to it. I do meditate every day. It really helps me to be so much less hyper. But I know my spirituality needs to be more. When I am in touch with it, it helps me be more focused and grounded, and I feel much healthier."

"So it sounds like you continue to work on your self and your relationships," I observe, starting to summarize.

"Absolutely. I feel very, very good about my work with the ideas for disentangling. It truly built a solid foundation upon which I expand in all of my therapy work since I was with you. I am busy using these ideas in improving relationships with my mother and father. In terms of my relationship with Thomas, I see my self wanting to make some very big changes that help me to have a greater capacity for intimacy. Disentangling helps me to find and develop my self and not get lost in the other person, but I am finding that I use it to keep my self at a distance from my husband when I don't necessarily want to."

I am struck by the importance of her comment. I agree with her. Disentangling is in some ways only a beginning. We cannot be healthy in a relationship if we have no clear, strong self. So disentangling can help us with this, if we are the ones prone to losing our self in others. There are, however, many important steps thereafter that our healthy self needs to take and to risk in order to cultivate healthy intimacy. It looks to me like once again my conversations with Lindsey are helping me to see new and exciting work that I want to do both personally and professionally.

Our hour is now up and both of us need to end the conversation and return to work with our clients. We agree we have enjoyed talking, and in many ways feel like we just talked last week, like little time has passed since her last therapy session with me.

"I'm *so* glad you called," Lindsey says. "I've just got to keep reminding my self of these things!"

# Trish

Trish graduated from college one year ago. I knew that she had returned to her hometown, and I strongly suspected that I could reach her through her parents' home. Sure enough, when I called their number, her voice was on the answering machine. I left her a general message asking her to call me back.

Trish called within the day, cheery and enthusiastic. She was quite aware of the work I have been doing to write this book, as she was active in a Disentangle Group when I first started writing. I told her that she was one of the clients I describe in the book and asked if she'd be willing to schedule a follow-up interview with me.

"Of course!" she responded.

We meet a week or so later in my office. She lives two hours away and has come for the day to visit friends and to speak with me. As with my other clients, I sent Trish her fictionalized case description and questionnaire in advance. In her usual way, Trish comes prepared for our session with journal entries she has done to help her answer my questions. Trish is quite a writer, and frequently uses that talent and passion to help her sort through her experiences and feelings so that she can work with them in therapy and life. Today is no exception.

"So how are you?" I ask.

"Hopeful. This past year has been hard for me. I have had a lot of growth and change and am hopeful that good things will happen in the future."

Trish explains some of the things that have made this last year difficult: problems with credits needed for graduation, loss of what was an unhappy job, and recently the loss of her best friend who met a guy and moved to another state. Trish is currently interviewing for a new job and trying to figure out what she really does want to be doing with her life now.

She continues positively, "You know, I'm a late bloomer. All that I've been through has made me more sensitive and more confrontational. When stuff happens, I'm able to brush my self off and go on. I've learned that when it comes to relationships, I have a choice as to whether to spend time with someone or not, whether to 'go there' with someone or not. And if they are unhappy with me about my choices, I can honestly say to my self about them, 'I don't care if you don't like me.'"

"That's quite a change," I remark. "It makes me think back to your relationship freshman year with Ashley. You said then you were so 'hooked' on her that you felt compelled to conform to what you thought she wanted you to be."

"That relationship slowly fizzled for me. It started ending by my taking away my illusion of her being a mysterious being and seeing her instead as a messed-up person. No offense intended to her. I just in my mind created a real fantasy about what her life was like, a life so exciting and risky and different from my own. In doing that, I could not see the truth about her problems and the crappy way she treated me. She calls now and then—it's just like talking to anyone else."

As Trish continues, it's obvious she's thought about this and has a lot to say.

"It also helped that I started going to Al-Anon meetings. The philosophies of Al-Anon and disentangling are so related. I learned through both of these sources to get the focus onto my self and to take it off of the person with whom I'm obsessed. And my black-and-white thinking turned to color. Things don't have to be all or nothing, a success or failure. I am not all bad or all good. I used to see everyone else as perfect, and I'm not. That's another sick illusion I've let go."

"I remember your relationship with your father was frustrating for you as well," I comment.

"Yes, it was. And it still can be. I've come to some acceptance of him as he is. He just doesn't have it to give to me, but I still have to work hard to detach and set boundaries with him. He wants to control everything, and he's good at guilt-tripping. I can still get unglued with him."

"So what do you do?" I ask.

"Well, I've learned ways to detach. I've learned that detachment isn't about not caring. Detachment allows me to care about my self and also care about the other person, but as separate entities, not intertwined. So I may detach by slowing down, being in the moment, physically leaving the room, choosing what I say carefully (not trying to control), and not losing my self in the interaction."

She continues, "And probably the single most important thing I ever learned is that it's not only okay, but *essential* to have personal boundaries and to enforce them. I know that it's time to set a boundary when I feel afraid, anxious, pissed off, or embarrassed. It's at those moments that I tell my self, 'I won't go there. I refuse to engage.'"

Returning specifically to her relationship with her father, Trish adds, "I can still feel not good enough for my dad, though those feelings have a little less power than in the past. But you know, when I'm centered I know that I'd rather be who I am than who he thinks I am."

"And how about spirituality in your life?" I ask.

"Spirituality has always meant a lot to me. I go to my church, attend Al-Anon, and use the 'Serenity Prayer.' I see God as my ally.

"Recently I went through a rough spot about God. I felt like a victim and kept asking, 'If you love me so much, why are you doing this to me?' Now I can accept life on life's terms and know in my bones that there was a lot He has been teaching me in the past year. I know that when I say, 'Not my way, but Your way,' things may not turn out as anticipated. I pray a lot and feel more connected to Him these days.

"I really know I can let go and let God," she adds.

"Anything else you want to comment on that was helpful to you in our disentangling work?" I ask as we start to wind down our interview.

"It was good to be in groups with people who were dealing with similar issues. I didn't always like or agree with all the people, but I found the companionship valuable. This is true for me in Al-Anon still."

There is then a comfortable quiet between us in the session. We agree we have said all that needs to be said now. We acknowledge how good it has been to see each other and to review in this way. Trish leaves with us knowing that our paths will likely cross again at some time and place.

Several days later I receive a note from Trish that reads:

> *It was so cool catching up with you today! As fate would have it, I got a job today. There was a message on my answering machine when I got home from our meeting. I start next week as the public relations person for a local resort. Isn't that ironic? I'm really excited!*

# Rebecca

Rebecca is now a high school senior. We still work together on a fairly regular basis, though the frequency of her appointments has diminished considerably. She will graduate this June and has been accepted into the college of her choice, much to her delight. She has received many honors at her high school and has many extracurricular activities that she cares about and enjoys. Rebecca is a serious and sincere young woman who is earnest about her interests and her relationships. She has high standards for her self and for others.

She stays today after her individual therapy session for yet another hour so we can talk through this follow-up interview for the book. She is so excited to be included in the book, because she is so excited about the work she is doing for her self.

"So how are you?" I begin, obviously referring in a comparative way to how she was two years ago when she and Ben broke up.

"I have survived more than anybody could imagine. I'm not exceptionally giddy or depressed. I see my self as in a transition time where I'm learning not to be dependent on drugs, sex, or medication."

"Tell me more about what you mean," I request.

"Well, when I was with Ben I was living in all sorts of false worlds. Back then I was into creating the situation that I wanted in my relationship. I would create it by giving and giving and giving and then hoping that it would be how I wanted it to be. I wanted to create a situation where he would love me so much!"

She continues, "I needed constant reassurance from him that he loved me and would not leave me. And our relationship was so 'extreme' in that we only had each other in our lives."

"So did you guys ever get back together?"

"No, not really," she responds. "We tried, or at least I tried, a bunch of different things but nothing brought us back together."

"So how did you deal with that and your feelings along the way?" I ask.

"Well, for a while I used more false things, like drugs, sex, 'temporary' things. Then I started making some progress in finding who I am and wanting to take care of me."

"Could you say more about finding your self, Rebecca? As you know, that's what disentangling is all about, and your comments may help our readers," I say.

"Well, as I said before, in the past I needed Ben to love me so much. I needed his constant reassurance. At some point I realized that often I simply was not thinking about things in terms of my self at all. So I began to practice paying attention to me instead of the extreme of always thinking of him and what I wanted from and with him. Now I love my self enough that I don't wholly rely on the love of someone else, and I give not to get what I want back, but give more freely without attachments."

"That can be very hard to do," I comment.

"No joke!" Rebecca replies.

"What helped you to make these difficult changes?" I ask.

"Well, certainly waking up to the reality that I was trying to create a relationship in the way that I wanted it to be and that didn't work.

"And learning to step back from the situation and see it more clearly. Now you know I have trouble doing that. I just want to keep believing that it can be the way I think it should be, but when I can get some distance I can find my bottom line, which is 'I can wait. I can just let things happen.'

"But getting to that place *is* really tough for me," she adds. "When I am in the midst of my situation, I have to work extremely hard with my self to back off, to let go."

"So what else can help then?" I ask.

"As I make these efforts to detach, what I think is that I want to reattach my self to me. I am falsely and problematically attached to the other person. If I can reattach to me, I can deal with disruptions, not freak out, and deal with the fact that I cannot control everything. It is hard for me to find the medium, to not go to extremes, but I tell my self that I can't control or solve everything now."

"Also," she continues, "I have to set boundaries with my self about all of this. I say things to my self like 'Don't you find any excuses to go by his house. Don't you pick up the phone if you are about to call him.' And also, I'm learning to 'not put up with their stuff.'"

"And what about spirituality, Rebecca? I know that you have been very active in your church over the years I have known you, and I wonder what role spirituality has in helping you with you."

"Well, as you know, I'm big on control. I've finally started to realize that in order to have the control I want, I have to let go of trying to have full control. This is where spirituality can help me. When I was with Ben, I thought he *was* God.

"Now, I am coming to know spirituality as a 'safe hold' for me. My spirituality is not defined by particular institutions; rather, I am learning to see it as a relationship between a higher being and my self that works within me and is not critical of me. This spiritual relationship provides a home for my soul."

She continues, "I am recognizing the importance of spirituality more now. I enjoy conversations about it; I feel more connected with it; and I do find it a challenge to use it to help me with my disentangling. My control stuff really wants to just step in there."

It is past time for us to stop our conversation. Rebecca and I have come to know each other well, and this topic is close to our hearts. We could say more, and we know it is time to end for now.

"As you live your life now, Rebecca, which of these elements of disentangling do you find most helpful for you?" I ask.

"Each of the elements is very important to me, and I find them to be interwoven. This is not a step one/step two process. I use each of them, with awareness or not, situation by situation. When I look back at something that happened, I can see, for example, how I detached, set some boundaries, and reminded my self of the reality of the situation.

"And Nancy," she adds, "I find disentangling more than 'helpful.' I find it to be a way of living that enables me to 'live happily ever after' if I tend to my self."

"There is nothing more important to me than my serenity."

# 9 The Next Twenty-or-So Years

*"There is nothing more important to me than my serenity. That's what motivates me the most to disentangle. I've learned that the serenity I lose in trying to make my point or have things my way is not worth it. I have come to know what serenity feels like, and that's what I want for me."*

*Nancy, age 48*

It's been two more years since I wrote the next-to-last chapter of this book. If I looked at my notes, I bet I'd find that it's been almost two years to the day.

It's time to write this last chapter. It's not past time to do so. I can feel it simply *is* time to do it.

I cannot explain the delay in finishing this book. In fact, I really don't think of it as a delay, so I'll dispense with that word. I have known all along that I would write it when I was ready. And I feel ready now.

Now, I sit by a pond in the Adirondack Mountains of New York. I am once again traveling with my husband, our daughter, and our dog Daisy. This morning Daisy and I have hiked out from our campsite early so she can get a walk and I can start this chapter. We walked through a deep, old pine forest to get here. As we walked on the bed of pine needles, through the quiet darkness of the woods, I thought it was like entering a sanctuary, a sanctuary to which I had come to start laying down these concluding words. Now we're both sitting here on those pine needles with the sound of running water and the sight of tall evergreen trees against a blue sky just past the pond. I am ready.

## Living in the Now

I notice how many times I have already used the word "now." That's a very important word for me when I think of what to say in this chapter entitled "The Next Twenty-or-So Years." I have come a long way in learning to live in the now. It has taken conscious practice for me to learn to do this. I have always been about planning, thinking ahead, looking forward to, worrying about. Or, I could fret about, keep going over, or wish I had done something different about things past. I can still live in these ways in a heartbeat. It is my awareness of these behaviors of mine and my intentional reconnecting with my breath, my spirit, and all that is within me and around me at the moment that help me to live in the now—which is where I want to be.

Living in the now greatly facilitates disentangling. For the most part, I am not entangled if I come back to the now. A lot of my entanglements involve projections into the future about what someone else's words or behaviors may ultimately mean or cause. And other entanglements involve my mixing what has happened to me in the past with what is happening now. Either way, adding the future and/or the past with the present is likely to buy me entanglements.

Living in the now also helps me to disentangle if, despite my best efforts, I still feel entangled. When I bring my self to the now, I can really hear what the other person is saying without adding my own twists. If I add my own twists, I can be aware of them, feel them, acknowledge them, and check them out with the other person, always coming back to now—over and over.

"So how is this playing out in your daily life?" you may ask.

"With progress," I am pleased to report, "slow but sure progress."

My husband, Monty, and I are still together and are consciously working on aspects of our relationship after twelve years of each of us working on our own self and experiencing considerable alienation and frustration in our marriage. Last month we were joking in the kitchen about something, and he put his arms around me and said, "I'm so glad I married you."

"That is amazing," was my candid response. And then I quickly noticed my use of the word "amazing," and I remembered the promises of AA (*Alcoholics Anonymous*, 1976, p. 83) which use the beautiful sentence: "If we are painstaking about this phase of our development, we will be amazed before we are halfway through." I moved my self to tears and awe at the moment and at my ability to be in the moment without trying to run from it or alter it.

What I am most aware of working on now in my relationship with Monty is simply listening and speaking. This past winter I did an amend with him. I couldn't have done it earlier. I wasn't ready. Until then I couldn't see my self as well. I wasn't clear or strong in my self. All of my work with disentangling, using the varied ideas in this book, however, has helped me greatly to find and cultivate my self, that self that was lost in someone else and is now found. She is here with me now, stronger, clearer, more well-defined, not well-defended.

So with these improvements, I was able to apologize to my husband for my contributions to our communication problems over the years.

I said, "I am sorry for the difficulties I have caused in our relationship. I know that many of the problems have come from my problems in communicating with you, and I know those problems have come from two particular aspects.

"One, I have had trouble receiving what you have wanted to tell me. I have frequently rejected what you had to say to me. I have been defensive and closed. I am sorry for this. It has made it impossible for you and me to truly communicate, interact, and grow by my cutting you off in so many ways so much of the time.

"Two, I have messed with our communication by not speaking up for my self to you in healthy, honest ways. The sending end of my communication patterns has also been very disturbed. I have not honestly told you what I am feeling, thinking, wanting, not wanting. I edit and qualify terribly. Much goes through my mind but not out my mouth. So how would you have known me? How could we have been really living in an honest, meaningful way? I am sorry for the damage this has caused to our relationship."

The whole time I was saying these things to him I was both scared and peaceful. To openly say them was amazing to me.

I couldn't believe I was doing it, and I could believe it. What I knew most of all was that as I was saying them, I repeatedly made conscious contact with my higher power. What a noticeable relief I felt each time I reminded my self of God's presence with me. This spiritual connection helped me to let go of the outcome of what I was saying and trust that what I was doing was what I was supposed to be doing, regardless of what followed.

This inner strength was born of my personal work with all that I am sharing here with you in this book. I had not been able to receive what my husband has to say to me because I have not had a strong enough self to receive it. I have been scared that if I let his stuff in, I would be destroyed. If I went with one of his suggestions or ideas, this would completely invalidate me. I have had to learn that he can say what he wants, and I can listen, consider, evaluate, keep, or throw out. Just because he says it, it doesn't have to be so. He never intended to imply that. I chose to hear him that way because of my insecurities about me. Now I'm not 100 percent, but I am a lot more aware of and responsive to me, so his input is much less threatening. In fact, I now often welcome it.

As for being better able to speak up for my self, this, too, is a product of my stronger self. I have been afraid to tell people, and especially my husband, what I really mean. I have been afraid that if I did, he would get mad at me and leave me. It's as simple as that. So I have been willing to try to control our relationship by only saying what I think will not rock the boat or keep him from abandoning the ship. What a false way to live. What a fake relationship that creates. And again, I must say that I have chosen to create all these abandonment fears. I have not been threatened with them. Now I am less afraid of someone being angry with me and leaving me. Those things may happen, and I will be okay. But more than likely, those things will not happen. Rather, my honesty will enable each of us to grow and to get to know each other more fully. And who knows where things will go from there?

So as I told you, I said these things to my husband as an amend. This is twelve-step program language, to speak of amends. An amend is not just an apology. An amend is saying you're sorry *and* saying that you are going to do some things so that it won't happen again as best as you are able. My amend to him was offered in this spirit. I am sorry for and tired of being defensive and dishonest. I am sorry for how it has affected me, and to that end, I offer the amend equally, if not more so, to my self and recommit again and again to freeing my self from these old ways of noncommunicating and living in unreal ways.

Though my anecdotal focus here has been on my relationship with my husband, I must add that I am practicing these changes in all of my relationships. My relationship with my husband has simply been a glaring opportunity for me to learn these things about my self and to grow in these ways that enable me to be more honest and centered with others.

In my relationship with our daughter, Grace, I bring my self over and over to being with her and me in the now. If I am thinking about what else I need to do while she and I are doing something or she is talking to me, I do not enjoy the moment nearly so much, and I miss the full pleasure of her company. Grace, who is nearly twelve now, has grown up as fast as I was warned she would. Time and our lives are speeding by. As I write this, we are visiting a friend who lives on Lake Ontario. We visited here five years ago. I have been walking around for the past couple of days muttering out loud and to my self, "I can't believe it's been five years since we were here!" I really can't. It scares me for my life to be moving on so quickly, and especially in terms of our daughter's growing. Last time we were here she was buying stuffed animals; now she's buying lip gloss. I don't want to miss any more than I have to miss of life with her. Being present with her, really present, is very important to me and to my way of living so that our lives aren't a blur and full of regrets of misspent time.

And as Grace is moving more toward adolescence with its accompanying struggles between dependence and autonomy, I am finding that my ideas for disentangling apply equally to my relating to her. In fact, if I don't use them, I am going to be in trouble with my self. One Wednesday night several months ago, right at bedtime, we got into a disagreement about something. We don't argue very often. We usually can talk things out. But with fatigue upon both of us, we came to an angry stalemate. I was starting to do my stuff, which is repeat, repeat, repeat my self and keep asking questions of her to try to make my point and move the conversation my way. Real mature, huh? I was entangling my self and nothing was being accomplished. So, I intervened on my own behalf (I was by far the bigger part of the problem) and said "good night."

When I went upstairs to my room, mentally bringing my self to disentangling/Al-Anon ideas and away from whatever we were arguing about (and I was already starting to feel bad about the whole scene), I thought, "I am so glad for being in Al-Anon. Much of what I am learning there is going to apply to my relationship with her as she becomes a teenager." And then, with both humor and seriousness, it came to me: We need a twelve-step group called Adol-Anon for family and friends of adolescents. Yes, living with a teenager can invite entanglements, too, and healthy relating to them can come from practicing such principles as detachment and boundaries in a dynamic way.

My life with Grace is great. I don't mean to say in any way that she is my guinea pig upon which I test these ideas. We are both different human beings, though, and sometimes we see things differently or want different things. It's at those points that the ideas for disentangling come forward more naturally now, and I use them to recenter me, to quiet me, to clarify me, and then to move forward in an acting, not reacting, way.

And good things are happening for me with my parents, too. I have been as afraid of speaking openly with them as I have with my husband. Over the years I have kept many things to my self, not wanting to upset or disappoint them. As I have become more centered and secure with my self, I have become more comfortable sharing the real me with them. In fact, I wanted to share more of the real me with them. I am feeling grateful that we all have lived as long as we have so that we can keep getting to know each other in more real ways.

Recently I had a problem and chose to call and talk with them about it. They listened and were supportive of me. They did not judge me, say "we told you so," or do any of the other things I feared they might say or do that would express their displeasure with me. My fears of having people angry at me and leaving me were my creations for the most part and have kept me captive for too long. It is time for me to move through those fears and into reality.

I know that I am also practicing these disentangling ideas in a wide variety of other relationships. Whether I am dealing with my disappointment in something my boss failed to do for me, trying to clarify billed services to an insurance company in order to get paid, or negotiating the return of an unsatisfactory item or service, I do best if I am mindful of me and any number of these disentangling ideas. I keep my center or retrieve my center, whichever it happens to be, so I can represent my self in ways I want to represent me.

And I have more real friendships in my life than ever before. I have met many of my close friends on this or a similar recovery path. I have not gone it alone. We are willing to honestly look and laugh at our self. We share our stories with each other and grow by doing so. The twelve-step programs call this sharing your experience, strength, and hope. I find it to be a great way to go. No one is telling me what to do. I'm not telling others what to do. And yet I'm getting a wealth of information to help me become more centered and whole. When I am with these friends, or even think of them, I feel like I am coming home. There is a familiarity and comfort that just can't be beat, a familiarity and comfort that soothes me and inspires me to further honesty and healing. I am glad and grateful to be me.

## Well-Defined by Me

That's it! That's one of the greatest gifts that has come to me through this journey of mine: I am glad and grateful to be me. I know me much better. I listen to me. I return to me over and over. I wander out into the old, familiar world of watching and waiting for others, of wondering what they're thinking, what they want, trying to tell them what is best for them, trying to fix what's not mine to fix—see how easily I can reel off this list? And then—I catch my self doing any number of these things and I return to me, a place even more soothing than being with close friends. I listen to what I feel and want, and oblige it if possible. I feel calmer, happier, and connected to the present.

In the past, I was not well-defined; I was well-defended. I was holding on for dear life to ideas of how I was and should be. Let anyone offer me criticism or friendly feedback, and I would feel threatened and defensive. I would not necessarily show these feelings in dramatic ways, but I knew they were there. And later, as the day wore on, those feelings would turn into self-doubt and worry. The defensiveness made it close to impossible for me to use the feedback in any constructive way and, interestingly enough, eroded my struggling self further.

In the past, I was well-defined by things outside my self: by external events and attributes, by my history of what I had done, by what other people said and did to me and how they reacted to me. My happiness and sense of self were based far more on relationships than I wanted to believe. They were based especially on the condition, or my perception of the condition, of my intimate relationship(s).

I am different than that now, when I am in good form.

I am now, at least, better defined by me.

A couple of years ago, a close friend of mine was unhappy with her relationship with her live-in partner. She knew well the difficulties I was having in my relationship with my husband, and yet she knew I was happy and growing in my life. I wrote the following notes shortly after my conversation with her, because I, too, was struck by my newfound ability to be doing well even though my intimate relationship was not.

*April 13, 1998—Huntington Beach, S.C.*

*On this past Saturday I was talking on the phone with Liz, a friend in need. She was angry and confused about her present relationship of six years. She's been working with her self to leave that relationship. Her partner had just given her u card stating his deep caring for my friend and his hopes that they were growing together in their relationship.*

*Liz was furious about receiving the card. The card was obviously "messing with my brain," she said. At first she blamed this on her partner, accusing him of being manipulative and throwing her a crumb now that he could see how Liz was backing off. Maybe so.*

*And maybe Liz's confusion was coming also from her self. And so we talked about it this way. The messages she was getting from her partner's card were very contradictory to the ones she's experiencing daily in their relationship. That contradiction upset Liz because it threw her off. It challenged what she thinks is her position and what may well be her position. It put a small hole in her present belief system that she needs to leave this relationship, and her insecurities were gushing out: "Maybe I don't want to leave him. What if I'm wrong? He's really a nice person sometimes. Maybe it's just me."*

*And so she was quite upset to feel all these assorted feelings and to have all these assorted thoughts again. She was very unhappy.*

*Liz said to me, "Nancy, I know we have similar experiences in our relationships. I've called you, in part, because I know you know what I'm talking about. If you don't mind, would you tell me how you find your happiness?"*

*Funny she should ask. Just this past Tuesday I had been almost overwhelmed with gratitude for things in my life as I drove my hour's drive to work up the Shenandoah Valley on a pretty spring day.*

*And so when Liz asked, the items were already there and waiting to be heard again:*

*I am happy that I have such a lovely daughter whom I love and who loves me and whose company I enjoy so much and who enjoys my company.*

*I am happy with my old clapboard home that faces a creek and a river and not a road.*

*I love the wildness of my yard and the amateur gardening I do around here.*

*I am happy that my parents have both lived as long as they have and that they are healthy enough to live in their own home, have us visit, and share our lives.*

*I am happy with my work, with my work colleagues, and with the freedom I have to schedule my self as I do and to take long trips with my family.*

*I am happy that I can travel and see places and people, happy that I was raised as a camper and so know how to travel on low budgets and do wonderful things.*

*I love that I have my health and that I have been able to be an amateur dancer all these years. I am at a great studio with a teacher and classes I love.*

*I have been extremely blessed with strong Al-Anon meetings near me, and I feel so at home with many of the members. It is truly a place I can be me comfortably.*

*I love my circle of friends here in the county. It is nice to spend these years together ruising our children, growing in our own lives, and just plain having fun.*

*I love my animals and value their companionship in my life.*

*I am happy that I am able to be by my self and have such a good time.*

*I am more confident about my self and my work and am feeling increasingly creative.*

*"I am a lucky lady, Liz."*

*And I meant that. There have been times over the years when I've been told to make a gratitude list, and I would, often half-heartedly. The idea of imposing gratitude on my unhappy feelings seemed fake and wrong. I'm sure it does have usefulness, though, and so I have done this type of listing at less happy times.*

*This list, however, came to me, and still does as I write, from real feelings of happiness, serenity, clarity, and gratefulness. And Liz could hear this. "You've more than answered my question. What you're telling me is that your happiness is not completely dependent on your relationship."*

*"That's right," I said. "It used to be that 90 percent of me was focused on, devoted to, pulling on, watching out for my relationship. Early on, when I heard people telling me to keep the focus on me and not on the alcoholic, I felt quite lonely. And I was. Without that focus on the other person, there was little else there for me. No wonder I was lonely — and resistant to looking to me."*

*"You've got it right there," Liz said. "That's what's come to me as you've talked, that I'm putting all my eggs into my partner's basket."*

*"Thanks," she said.*

*"Thank you," I said, grateful to have times where I do see and experience my own good feelings.*

And over the years of writing this book, some fabulous sentences have come out of the mouths of my clients that describe this learning to define our self through our own internal processing rather than through the external demands, expectations, and pressures of others or through the condition of our intimate relationships. Sometimes clients have only been in therapy a matter of weeks before they are uttering these statements of insight and freedom. I am amazed and charmed at their quick progress and sharp accuracy. They are bright and intuitive people who, upon taking some type of break from their conflicted relationships, are able to see how they have lost their self and what they want to do about it.

## On **Facing Illusions:**

*"I thought I had to live with it, but I don't."*

*"I was grieving for what I thought was."*

*"The person I was married to only exists in my mind."*

*"The whole marriage was a lie."*

*"My eyes are clear."*

*"I do realize I let things decide how I'm going to feel."*

*"I'm feeling uneasy about the way I used to feel. I wasn't clear-headed. I wonder if he drugged me."*

## On **Detaching:**

*"I can't make him better."*

*"It's a free world out there. You don't let your family rule who you see."*

*"I've not done anything wrong."*

*"I didn't care if I didn't have anything."*

*"She's always in the back of my mind. . . . I can't help her. . . . I wish I could. . . . I wish she'd admit to her problems. . . . I can't let that bother me."*

*"I'm working on letting go of his stuff. I'm not going to let this bother me."*

*"I feel like I let him down. I thought I could turn him around."*

## On **Setting Healthy Boundaries:**

*"I just knew it was right [to leave] . . . back there doing my same old routine . . . like a nursemaid."*

*"I've changed: I'm saying exactly what I feel."*

*"I wanted to call and tell him, but it would have riled me up more."*

*"I'm tired of being the giver all the time."*

*"I'm going to write my self a letter to remind my self . . ."*

*"I don't want my life modified for some lowlife."*

*"I need to learn to express my self to others."*

*"I can really hear him talk. I realized I need to slow down and listen."*

*"I have my limits."*

*"I kept my mouth shut. I didn't let it bury me."*

*"I did not want her to be there. She would offer me no comfort."*

On **Developing Spirituality:**

*"Nothing I could do about nothing."*

*"Disentangling has really given me the tools to live my life by the word of God."*

*"I can really only rely on my self and God."*

*"I see God as my ally."*

*"Entanglements are always there if we are not conscious."*

# Quietly Be. Quietly See.

I sit here in a coffeehouse in Charlottesville, Virginia, on a sunny Friday afternoon. It is March 9, 2001. I am here to enjoy my afternoon by writing. Perhaps I will finish this book.

I have just reviewed the list of quotations from my clients in the previous section. I am particularly struck by one as I start to write this last essay.

"Entanglements are always there if we are not conscious," says a dear and wise client of mine. Yes, my experience is that I can get caught up in someone or something fairly easily despite my work with my self on this. Only by being in the present with my feelings, thoughts, and experiences can I catch my self when I'm about to fall into my "stuff" or perhaps already have. This is the consciousness of which my client speaks. With this consciousness I can then work with my self to regain and retain my center.

And I make contact with my higher power to help me with this centering process as well. If I only apply ideas from facing illusions, detachment, and boundaries, I am still subject to my will and my issues of control. Using my self-will and self-control, I can still try to manage and control others and my self to meet my new goals of disentanglement. I can still get caught up in holding onto something, like my hopes of how I am becoming, rather than simply doing my part and then letting go to the flow of life. It is only by the addition of the spiritual parts of this process that I am transformed into a more peaceful and centered soul, letting it happen as it is to happen.

When I prepared the quotations from my clients in the previous section, I noticed that there were fewer quotations from which to select related to spiritual growth. I believe many of these clients are experiencing spiritual changes in their lives and yet have plenty of room to grow in their awareness of the spiritual aspects and the depth of their beliefs and faith.

This is true for me, too.

Over and over I catch my self about to say or do something to force a solution.

Just recently I once again observed this in my self. For the twenty billionth time I was trying to create a conversation with my husband. There was no problem afoot as far as I was aware, so it wasn't like I was going to say things to try to make things okay again (like I can do that anyway). We were just hanging out in front of the television at the end of the day. Consciously or unconsciously I decided I wanted some contact with him. So I started asking mundane questions, which he politely and succinctly answered with one-word responses. I could feel my self getting irritated at his not joining me in the ways I would have had it, so I applied some detachment and excused my self to go to bed with a not-so-great spirit.

The next morning as I drove my self to work, I was thinking about these events from the past evening and realized how I was trying to make things the way I wanted them to be. I wanted my husband to show interest in me and my day. I wanted him to pay attention to me and not to the television. I wanted to know he was glad to see me. I wanted some contact with him. I could not make any of this happen. It was not in my control, and I had set my self up by having these hopes and expectations.

It then came to me that I just need to "quietly be."

You would think that I would have this down pat by now, but I don't.

Quietly be.

Now that's a nice thought. I wrote it down on a slip of paper and have kept it close ever since.

Quietly be. Just sit. Be present. Be present with my self and the situation. Allow life to flow. Perhaps a conversation will come. Perhaps I will just enjoy being and being in the presence of someone else. Whatever I seek may already be. Whatever I need is probably already there. Quietly be, Nancy, with what is.

Several weeks later, as I awoke from my night's sleep, the phrase "quietly see" came to me. I knew right away that this was the piece that follows from quietly being. As I quietly be, I become aware of all sorts of things, good and bad, pleasing and disturbing. I work not to judge them but I do see them and experience them.

How different this is than being entangled and trying to force solutions. When I am doing those things, I can't and/or won't see things as they are. In fact, my entangled behaviors are efforts not to experience and see things as they are, but rather to make them as I believe they should be.

So now I "quietly be and quietly see." And I know that in so doing I am opening my self to the spiritual realm of my life. I couldn't even do this resigning-from-my-efforts-to-control if I didn't believe that there is a power greater than my self with me and in me. I know that my forcing things is my acting like I know what is best for me and others. When I let this forcing go, I let go to God with excitement and eager anticipation about how things are now and what is to come.

Who knows what the next twenty-or-so years have in store for me?

I do know I am looking forward to how my life unfolds over those years, living one day at a time, quietly being, quietly seeing, and keeping in conscious contact with my higher power.

"What is it that you are working on for your self?"

# Epilogue

Ten of "the next twenty-or-so years" have already passed since I first completed *Disentangle*. It is now June, 2010, and I have been tasked with writing an epilogue to bring you, the reader, up to date in the present. Central Recovery Press and I thought this might be useful since I have had the opportunity of having some years of presenting, teaching, and living with the material in *Disentangle*.

I am glad to continue this story. Some of this story, the parts about marketing, development, and presentations and *Disentangle*'s publication by CRP, are told in the Preface to this second edition. I will continue the story here, looking at my work with the book's material with individuals and with my self.

In addition to professional presentations and extended workshops in the broader world, I have, over these years, offered *Disentangle* in rich and more intimate settings—settings in which its material continues to be used and developed. These would be the settings where I can comment on "Others on This Journey" over these ten years. These Others include individuals in an ongoing Disentangle Group as well as participants in a Codependence Camp inspired by the book.

I have continued to offer a Disentangle Group through my private practice. This group meets once every two to three months and provides continuing support for its members who have studied and worked with the *Disentangle* material. The format for each group is open and yet known. Initially I present some new ideas to enrich our work in developing a healthy self, and/or I review or have us practice something we have learned in the past. The members then have time to talk, clarifying what they need and want from our time together and venting and sorting and gaining insight.

Over the years, these Others have definitely improved in their sense of self. Each of them seems to have a clearer sense of self and a stronger sense of self. Yes, they still can get entangled. So can I. Their mission, though, is to notice their entanglements and respond with less reactive behaviors and more centered behaviors that reflect their true self. Our gatherings continue to help them to hear and know that true self. "I" statements abound in our sessions, as do statements of the reality of the particular situations and boundaries they need to continue to assert. Frequently we use mindfulness practices to quiet our selves so that we can better access our spiritual self. Group members often cite twelve-step programs and their churches as continuing sources of spiritual development.

In addition to this group, I have had the deep pleasure of working with individuals on this material at what we call our Codependence Camp. Shortly after *Disentangle* was first released, a mental health therapist visiting my community found the book in the local bookstore. After reading the book, she was so excited about its contents that she contacted me to see if I was willing to come to her part of Virginia to do a workshop on the book. Of course I was! And I did. The day there with the participants was lovely.

After the workshop, that therapist, now a good friend, said that she had always thought of having retreats there at her home where we had done the workshop. It is a charming place in the spirit of a bed-and-breakfast. She said, "Maybe we could have something like a Codependence Camp." I thought the idea was just great, and we have pursued it quite compatibly. We have now had ten camps. We offer them twice a year and are able to have eight to ten campers each time. We have developed a regular following of campers who intentionally save the camp dates and return to work on their self. These campers are also Others on This Journey.

The camp has been a wonderful place for me to deepen and extend my work with *Disentangle*. I love preparing the agendas for camp. At the end of each camp it is usually pretty clear what we want to focus on in the next camp, and I get to consider those topics, find additional resources for us, and learn lots more my self. Once we are at camp, I facilitate most of the sessions, and I get to experience how the campers are working with the material presented and how it applies to them.

Camp is designed as a place to actively practice self-awareness and self-care. If you need time for your self, please take it. If you have something you need to share, please do so. Be mindful of trying to please others to the exclusion of your self. Over and over, come back to you and respond accordingly, using the skills and resources you have been learning.

And camp is good for me—not only because of all the ways I get to work with my *Disentangle* material, but also because I get to practice it my self as a presenter and as a human being. I try to do all of the exercises and assignments I give to the campers, and each time I leave camp with new insights and goals.

You may be thinking, "Be specific. Exactly what has happened for you, Nancy, over these ten years? What is it that you are working on for *your* self?"

I'll start by giving you a snapshot of my life since I wrote Chapter Nine, "The Next Twenty-or-So Years," in 2000. My husband and I continue to be together, and we each continue to be in recovery. Some days our relationship is challenged by differences between us and the ways we each present and pursue those differences. Some days when this happens, my own recovery is challenged, and I can regress to unnecessary neediness or anger. And we have survived as a couple. And sometimes we can even thrive as a couple. There are many ways we are compatible and many ways we learn things from each other. I know I have grown tremendously by having a marriage with Monty. This book speaks to many of those things learned.

Our daughter, Grace, is now twenty-one years old. She just graduated from college with a degree in sculpture and extended media. She is also a fashion designer. She combines all of these interests and talents into making wearable art. She is highly skilled in her designs and construction and has already won many awards. She plans to enter graduate school in Chicago in the fields of fashion and wearable art in the summer of 2011.

Grace is a lovely soul, and Monty and I and Grace still really enjoy being together when we can. Monty and I have been able to work together as parents of Grace. We have valued consistency, fairness, and good communication among all of us. We have really tried to help Grace grow into the person she is, not the person we think or want her to be. To this end, we have used many of the ideas in this book to raise her, encouraging her to think for her self and to be able to assert her self in acceptable ways. I have always said to Grace, "You can say anything you would like to me. It just has to be in a tone that I can accept." I have wanted her to know and develop her self, and I am sure that is happening.

And in the year 2006, we connected with my stepdaughter—Monty's daughter, Ava. She is forty years old. Actually, Grace, then a college freshman, made this possible by finding Ava through the Internet. I cannot tell this story of losing and finding Ava here and now. It is a narrative of its own. I will say that Grace and I had only met her once previously, when Grace was four years old. Ava came to visit us for several days. We had had no contact with her prior to that visit and had no contact afterward until Grace and Ava reconnected in 2006.

What is most important about this Ava story is that she is now in our lives in a rich and involved way. I have said that I sent one daughter off to college and two came home. What a great sentence! What a great experience! What a dream come true!

Another important aspect to this story is that her absence over these years and our not knowing her does reflect family dysfunction and alienation in many of the characters in this story. Again, I won't continue this story now. My intent here is to emphasize that recovery in our house has involved slowly coming to understandings of what happened, allowing feelings to be expressed and heard, and getting to know each other in honest, meaningful ways. I cannot imagine how we could be growing so well as a reunited family without our recovery.

All of this family action continues to happen at our home on the river here in the Shenandoah Valley of Virginia. Dogs and cats abound with us. Occasionally we do some work on this old house which we love, and occasionally we simply argue about the work that needs to be done on it. I garden, play in the river, and marvel that I have been given the opportunity to live in such a simple, charming getaway place.

For all the personal and interpersonal challenges I meet daily, I can say that I have truly been blessed with my home and my family. My mother is now eighty-six years old and is able to still live on her own in the home in which I grew up. She enjoys good health and a strong spirit for life. She is helped by my brother who lives near to her and who is able to be with her on a daily basis. He is a kind soul who loves taking care of her and our family's land. I visit them as often as I can and have come a long way in being comfortable with the ways we are all different from each other. I am able to listen to them and not lose my self in their beliefs and ways—which are not wrong, just different from mine. And I am able to share my views with them. I know what I can and cannot control and can and cannot fix: I can control *me*. I can fix *me*.

I am fixing me day by day.

I am careful to notice if I am falling to some *illusion*. Am I not seeing the reality of something? Of someone? Of my self? Am I carrying hope too far? Am I expecting things to be different and still getting the same results? Can I live with the reality I am finding? If I keep getting mad or sad about something, have I slipped back into believing something that isn't real? These are important questions I ask my self. I want to see things as they are in real time and not fool my self. This level of honesty can be grim and disappointing, and I know it can be freeing. I have felt that freedom and I like it.

I *detach* whenever it is necessary, whenever I am aware that I could fall into reacting rather than conscious acting. I don't get this perfect every time. Sometimes I do just react to something said or done. Right after I have reacted, I am aware that my serenity is now gone, and I don't like that feeling. So I try to pause, breathe, and listen before I respond.

The line-down-the-page that I present in the section on Detaching is infinitely useful to me. I am a visual person, meaning I do well to have at least a mental picture to help me understand something. The line-down-the-page helps me in this way. I imagine this line between my self and the other person. It is a vertical line drawn through space that separates us. The line is not a wall. It is simply a demarcation between where I end and the other person begins. We are, in fact, different people. With this in mind, when I go to suggest, offer, or ask something of this person on the other side of the line, I know it is important for me to go to the line and leave my suggestion, offer, or request there on the line. The other person then has the space and freedom to come to the line, examine what I have put there, and then respond for his or her self. Any efforts I make to push my agenda across the line or pull the other person across the line into my side leave me at increasing risk of losing my self. I have come a long way in learning to stay on my side of the line and not press as much into another's side of this boundary.

I work on *boundaries* all the time: boundaries with time, boundaries with people, boundaries with ideas and plans for the day, boundaries with what I can and cannot accept from others, boundaries with self. I am a handful for me to manage. I am full of ideas, hopes, dreams, conversations, inspirations. I have become aware that I will never in this lifetime be able to do all the things I want to do and to create. I am not discouraged by this at all. It just makes me more aware of the importance of my paying attention to the choices I make about how to use my self and the time I have.

For several Codependence Camps we worked on boundaries. I had thought we would have one camp on this topic. We ultimately had three camps on boundary setting. That was telling in terms of how challenging this area of work is for disentangling one's self. At one of those camps we used creative arts to help our self define our boundaries. Using felt, I made a small banner on which I made a collage from magazine pictures and words of what I want my life to look like. The pictures and words conveyed Good Marriage, Good Deals, Taste of Home, Traveling with Good Taste, and Break.

What was more important to this creation, though, was that I set up some numbers to help me with my limit setting so that these dreams of mine were more likely to become reality. I certainly did not want to fall into some illusion about living such a fine life. So interspersed in this collage are the numbers one, five, six, and eight. Each number has its own meaning to me: I want to get eight hours of sleep each night, see only six clients per day, and spend at least one hour each day with my husband talking and being together. To this day, I cannot remember what the five stands for. What does that tell you about my mental health? Well, it tells me there is some boundary out there I am not yet willing to see, absorb, and take seriously. Meanwhile, I have plenty to keep working on with my eight, six, and one. I regularly keep these numbers in mind as I make my boundary decisions daily.

As for *spirituality,* I feel so much more connected to my spiritual self than I did ten years ago. A primary reason for this growth is that my earlier work in recovery awakened me to the presence and importance of a power greater than my self. In my day-to-day life, prior to recovery, I had not even thought of letting go of things beyond my control. I had not thought of including my higher power so consciously in my thoughts and activities. I was just busy running my own life and the lives of others. This spiritual awakening has truly remained with me and grown.

The practicing of mindfulness has continued to help me a great deal in this spiritual growth. My ability to quiet my mind and return, over and over, to the present moment is a wonderful gift, a gift obtained through the regular practice of paying attention to the activities of my mind and returning my focus to the sensations within me and around me. This mindfulness then enables me to feel more spacious and lets in many wonders, including the wonders of understandings and experiences I could never have created for my self. When I am tangled and intent, I am tight, closed, and hanging on. When I practice mindfulness, I am open, loose, quiet, and free. This freedom is the door that opens me to increased spirituality.

In the spirit of this calm openness, I am living more and more in the flow of life. I am not always there, and I sure know when I am. When I am in the flow of life, things go smoothly and easily. I am not trying to make something happen. I am not trying to make someone do something. Instead, through my quietly being and quietly seeing, the next thing happens or not and opens or not. I do my part and let go. I quietly be and quietly see some more, and on my life goes, connecting with and trusting my spiritual self.

As part of my spiritual path, I also choose to attend church on a semiregular basis. Most of my life I have been searching for a church in which I feel at home. I can have trouble with some of the doctrine I hear, and I don't always agree with the positions churches take on particular issues. And yet I continue being a seeker. For the past twelve years I have attended a Protestant church in my community. I am recently encouraged about it as an additional source of my spiritual growth. There is realnes about what is being said and done there now, an increasing sense of inclusion and community, and an excellent weekly opportunity to intentionally quiet me and connect with my higher power.

Without any doubt, both *Disentangle* and I continue to be works in progress.

After coming off the river here in front of our house several days ago with Monty, I realized that my progress showed through to me by the way we had spent time together there. Our twenty-eight-year relationship has often involved being on the river, whether that has meant tubing or canoeing or swimming or just hanging out there. We have always had a canoe and have used it for trips of various lengths. Over the years, Monty has periodically proposed that we get two kayaks instead of one canoe. A major reason for this suggestion is that kayaks are much lighter and thus easier to get down to the river.

Until recently, I have never liked the idea of the kayaks. I did not want to be that separate from Monty. I am not afraid to handle a canoe or kayak by my self. I can do that. I have even been in the stern of a canoe for a couple of river races. My deal had to do with my entanglements, my not wanting to be separate from Monty and his experiences even there on the river. He might get ahead of me; he might have fun without me; he might even "leave" me. So I have never jumped on the kayak bandwagon. That together-and-yet-separate experience was not what I was wanting.

And yet here, the other day, that is exactly what I realized we have evolved to without any effort on each of our parts. .ast year I gave Monty an inflatable kayak for his birthday. I .ust openly acknowledge that I wanted it for me as much as .thing. Last year I also bought a ridiculously comfy lounge float for my self. It is the type usually used in a swimming pool with its own back rest and drink holder. This is not the type of flotation device you usually see on the river.

So the other day, Monty and I left the dogs in the house and took time for our selves on the river, Monty in the kayak and me on the lounging float. We traveled together. We traveled separately. We talked. We were quiet. I explored places of interest to me. He did his own exploring. It was an extremely pleasant time for me. I loved my separateness and freedom, and I loved his company. I was not afraid of missing out or losing. I was happy with my world and my experiences, which included him but were not based on him. The sky was blue, the mountains were clear, and spirit flowed. What a picture of health for me in those moments.

As I let *Disentangle* out into the bigger world where it can reach more people like you, who knows what will happen? And that question raises the very question that I pose at the end of Chapter Nine and to which I respond. I like that question and my response so much that I have often quoted my self, and now, still standing by it strongly, I choose, ten years later, to end again with the same words:

Who knows what the next twenty-or-so years have in store for me?

I *do* know I am looking forward to how my life unfolds over those years, living one day at a time, quietly being, quietly seeing, keeping conscious contact with my higher power, and then, with all of this in mind and heart, doing what I have come to know is best for me.

"Life is too short to be hurt by others."

# Characteristics of an Adult Child of an Alcoholic

1.  Adult children of alcoholics guess at what normal behavior is.

2.  Adult children of alcoholics have difficulty following a project through from beginning to end.

3.  Adult children of alcoholics lie when it would be just as easy to tell the truth.

4.  Adult children of alcoholics judge themselves without mercy.

5.  Adult children of alcoholics have difficulty having fun.

6.  Adult children of alcoholics take themselves very seriously.

7.  Adult children of alcoholics have difficulty with intimate relationships.

8.  Adult children of alcoholics overreact to changes over which they have no control.

9.  Adult children of alcoholics constantly seek approval and affirmation.

10. Adult children of alcoholics usually feel that they are different from other people.

11. Adult children of alcoholics are super responsible or super irresponsible.

12. Adult children of alcoholics are extremely loyal, even in the face of evidence that the loyalty is undeserved.

13. Adult children of alcoholics are impulsive. They tend to lock themselves into a course of action without giving serious consideration to alternative behaviors or possible consequences. This impulsivity leads to confusion, self-loathing, and loss of control over their environment. In addition, they spend an excessive amount of energy cleaning up the mess.

From the book *Adult Children of Alcoholics, Expanded Edition* by Janet Geringer Woititz. Copyright 1983 Janet G. Woititz. Published by arrangement with Health Communications, Inc. pp. xxvi–xxvii.

# Roles in an Alcoholic Family

## System Dynamics of the Alcoholic Family

| Motivating feeling | Identifying symptoms | Payoff | | Possible price |
|---|---|---|---|---|
| | | For individual | For family | |
| **DEPENDENT** | | | | |
| Shame | Chemical use | Relief of pain | None | Addiction |
| **ENABLER** | | | | |
| Anger | Powerlessness | Importance; self-righteousness | Responsibility | Illness; "martyrdom" |
| **HERO** | | | | |
| Inadequacy; guilt | Overachievement | Attention (positive) | Self-worth | Compulsive drive |
| **SCAPEGOAT** | | | | |
| Hurt | Delinquency | Attention (negative) | Focus away from dependent | Self-destruction; addiction |
| **LOST CHILD** | | | | |
| Loneliness | Solitariness; shyness | Escape | Relief | Social isolation |
| **MASCOT** | | | | |
| Fear | Clowning; hyperactivity | Attention (amused) | Fun | Immaturity; emotional illness |

Reprinted by permission of the author(s) and publisher: *Another Chance,* 2nd ed., Sharon Wegscheider-Cruse, Science & Behavior Books, Inc., p. 86.

"Breath of fresh air is in my head."

Al-Anon Family Group Headquarters, Inc. (1981). *Detachment* (brochure). New York, NY: Author.

*Alcoholics Anonymous* (1976). New York, NY: Alcoholics Anonymous World Services, Inc.

American Psychiatric Association. (1994). *Diagnostic and Statistical Manual of Mental Disorders* (4th ed.). Washington, DC: Author.

Beattie, M. (1987). *Codependent No More.* Center City, MN: Hazelden.

Cermak, T. L. (1986). *Diagnosing and Treating Co-Dependence.* Minneapolis, MN: Johnson Institute Books.

Drews, T. R. (1980). *Getting Them Sober, Volume 1.* South Plainfield, NJ: Bridge Publishing, Inc.

Drews, T. R. (1992). *Getting Them Sober, Volume 4.* Baltimore, MD: Recovery Communications, Inc.

Kabat-Zinn, J. (1990). *Full Catastrophe Living.* New York, NY: Delacorte Press.

Kabat-Zinn, J. (1994). *Wherever You Go, There You Are.* New York, NY: Hyperion.

*Merriam-Webster's Collegiate Dictionary* (10th ed.). (1998). Springfield, MA: Merriam-Webster, Inc.

Nhat Hanh, T. (1976). *The Miracle of Mindfulness: A Manual on Meditation.* Boston, MA: Beacon Press.

Nicholi, A. M., Jr. (1980). *The Harvard Guide to Modern Psychiatry* (5th ed.). Cambridge, MA: Harvard University Press.

Norwood, R. (1986). *Women Who Love Too Much.* New York, NY: Pocket Books.

Wegscheider-Cruse, S. (1989). *Another Chance: Hope and Health for the Alcoholic Family.* Palo Alto, CA: Science & Behavior Books, Inc.

Woititz, J. G. (1983). *Adult Children of Alcoholics, Expanded Edition.* Pompano Beach, FL: Health Communications, Inc.

control

> controlling behaviors 30, 42, 50, 51, 83, 109, 178

convincing 142

# D

defending 2, 82, 143, 168

defensiveness 146, 222

denial 82, 83

detaching 39, 79, 86, 88, 91, 92, 93, 95, 96, 106, 108, 111, 150, 227, 239

*Diagnostic and Statistical Manual of Mental Disorders (4th Ed.)* 50, 52, 249

Disentangle Groups 190, 193, 199, 203, 233, 234

disentangling 28, 31, 42, 43, 45, 47, 48, 51, 53, 54, 55, 56, 59, 61, 62, 64, 65, 67, 80, 100, 113, 123, 126, 147, 150, 162, 165, 169, 173, 175, 176, 177, 185, 186, 187, 191, 193, 195, 196, 201, 202, 205, 206, 208, 210, 211, 214, 216, 219, 220, 240

Drews, Toby Rice 75

# E

emotional distance/separation *See* detaching

entanglements 2, 23, 24, 37, 51, 56, 61, 72, 75, 80, 81, 84, 87, 88, 89, 110, 119, 120, 123, 145, 149, 150, 160, 169, 170, 171, 173, 194, 214, 215, 219, 234, 242

expectations 7, 49, 54, 65, 66, 82, 109, 191, 226, 230

extraction *See* disentangling

extremes 56, 58, 101, 209

# F

faith 19, 41, 62, 63, 150, 151, 170, 175, 177, 178, 179, 229

fantasies *See* illusions

fixing others 94

Four Areas of Work 45, 79

*Full Catastrophe Living* 162, 249

# G

*Getting Them Sober, Volume 1* 75, 249

gratitude list 225

guilt 25, 48, 96, 101, 129, 130, 150, 188, 195, 205

# H

Hanh, Thich Nhat 137

higher power

> developing a relationship with 171

> discovering 62, 169

> maintaining a relationship with 171, 172

# Q

questions  19, 24, 40, 47, 60, 65, 88, 99, 101, 105, 120, 124, 125, 126, 132, 133, 136, 192, 203, 219, 230, 238

quiet mind  162

# R

relaxation  153

# S

saying things once *See* brevity

self-esteem  50

self-talk  102

separating  viii, 60, 92, 93

serenity  iv, v, 37, 42, 55, 61, 64, 69, 72, 80, 87, 94, 109, 151, 154, 176, 212, 213, 225, 239

serenity prayer  109, 206

silence  41, 71, 101, 151, 153, 166, 167, 168, 171

simplify  41, 154, 166

  slowing down  117, 119, 126, 205

solitude  157, 158, 159

spiritual growth  61, 64, 67, 150, 229, 241

spirituality  iv, 9, 18, 39, 41, 61, 64, 67, 69, 72, 150, 151, 152, 155, 157, 161, 166, 169, 170, 171, 175, 176, 177, 179, 180, 181, 190, 194, 198, 202, 206, 210, 240, 241

staying in the present *See* present moment

sticking to the topic  133, 136

support groups  76

# T

truth  19, 39, 81, 82, 83, 84, 117, 204, 245

Twelve-step/fellowship/ meetings/programs  17, 18, 60, 61

# W

Wegscheider-Cruse, Sharon  26, 89, 90, 91, 247, 250

Woititz, Janet  88, 89, 91, 128, 131, 246, 250

women who love too much  108

# About the Author

**Nancy L. Johnston** is a Licensed Professional Counselor and Licensed Substance Abuse Treatment Practitioner in private practice in Virginia. She has a BS in Psychology from the College of William and Mary and an MS in Counseling Psychology from Virginia Commonwealth University.

With thirty-three years of clinical experience, she has developed these ideas from both her professional and personal experiences. Nancy specializes in treating adolescents and adults. She works with a wide range of emotional and behavioral issues, and she has always had a special interest in addiction and its effects on both individuals and family systems.

Nancy lives with her husband and daughter in an old house on a river in the Shenandoah Valley of Virginia.